TAKE CHARGE ~ IN BUSINESS

"In today's business environment, mental fitness has become a match-winning factor. The *Take Charge of Your Mind* 'full-brain workout' method will help your organization achieve a competitive advantage. It is a pragmatic on-the-job tool to develop finesse and mastery in the vital area of mind management."

– Alexander Brochier, VP Human Resources:
Information Management Group

"I tested a number of mind-management methods to reduce stress and be more creative. The *Take Charge* 'focus-phrase' method is the best – its efficient format, if practiced daily, will yield very real results . . ."

– D. Carl Long, CEO: Cityvision Systems

Beyond managing traditional resources, it's time to manage our most important resource – our mental potential. In my opinion the *Take Charge* programs provide the optimum methodology for tapping the higher potential of our mind-resource at work."

– Carlos Moreno, CIO, Skandia Germany

"Speaking as an experienced trainer and coach, I can say that the 'Take Charge' method is the most simple yet highly-effective tool available. There is no one in today's work-culture who can afford NOT to use this program."

– Otto Richter, President and Founder:
Human Holographics Inc.

"Going through a challenging year, I trained my management team in the *Take Charge* method. My people now feel less tense and stressed, and more creative and friendly – and there is much more power in the company."

    *– **Oliver Barth**, CEO of Satoris Inc (USA, Europe, China)*

"From my executive-coaching perspective, the *Take Charge* process is extremely effective. The daily method provides a major source of balance and strength, helping executives become both happier and more successful."

    *– **Christina Kuenzle,** Executive Coaching Firm Choice Ltd.*

"The *Take Charge* book, website, and personal coaching program help my employees experience the power of their own minds, gain more satisfaction at work, and contribute more fully to our company's success."

    *– **Ernstfried Prade,** Founder and President*
of Prade Design Inc.

"*Take Charge of Your Mind* is an essential ergonomic tool for 21st century organizations. The highly-accessible techniques and core exercises will decrease stress and enhance individual performance for even the most competitive corporate athlete."

    *– **Lucy Demian,** Executive Vice President,*
Eco Photon Consulting

TAKE CHARGE ~ IN MEDIA, EDUCATION, AND HEALTH

"As a therapist and media-personality expert I am impressed with the programs taught in *Take Charge of Your Mind,* where sound psychological principals generate breakthrough techniques and an expanded sense of purpose, direction, and great positive energy."

> – *Richard Levak Ph.D., clinical psychologist and head psychological consultant for Donald Trump's TV show* The Apprentice, *and* The Survivors

"When directing and producing for film and television, I apply the *Take Charge* method to perceive and perform at higher levels, and approach my work from a new expanded angle."

> – *Ingrun Finke, Founder and President of Finke Productions*

"Even a veteran seen-it-all psychologist and journalist like myself can marvel at *Take Charge*'s simple authority, usefulness and pleasures. The *Take Charge* program has the great benefit of being both easy to use – and profound."

> – *Jay Levin, founder of the prize-winning* LA Weekly *and* RealTalk LA *magazines*

"In the non-stop challenge of running my high school, I rely on the methods taught in *Take Charge of Your Mind* to navigate through each day's new challenges, make more conscious decisions, and remain balanced in difficult situations."

— ***David Mireles***, *Headmaster of Kula High School*

"From my experience as a medical doctor and educator, John Selby and Paul Hannam have developed a much-needed scientifically-based approach to help us connect with the greater integrative and healing power of the mind. When used as a daily routine, this method will reduce stress and thus improve health."

— ***Raymond A. Long***, *MD FRCSC Orthopedic Surgeon*

TAKE CHARGE

CHARGE

OF YOUR

MIND

Core Skills to Enhance Your Performance,
Well-Being, and Integrity at Work

Paul
HANNAM & SELBY

John

HAMPTON ROADS
PUBLISHING COMPANY, INC.

Cover design by Marjoram Productions
Cover art by Jonathan Friedman

Hampton Roads Publishing Company, Inc.
1125 Stoney Ridge Road
Charlottesville, VA 22902

434-296-2772
fax: 434-296-5096
e-mail: hrpc@hrpub.com
www.hrpub.com

If you are unable to order this book from your local
bookseller, you may order directly from the publisher.
Call 1-800-766-8009, toll-free.

Library of Congress Cataloging-in-Publication Data

Hannam, Paul.
  Take charge of your mind : core skills to enhance your performance,
well-being, and integrity at work / Paul Hannam and John Selby.
     p. cm.
  Summary: "Take Charge of Your Mind offers meditations for shifting out of
negative states of mind, along with simple 'focus phrases' for activating your
full awareness and potential, thereby improving productivity, problem-solving,
creativity, and leadership"--Provided by publisher.
  ISBN 1-57174-467-3 (6 x 9 tc : alk. paper)
  1. Success in business--Psychological aspects. 2.
Performance--Psychological aspects. 3. Attitude (Psychology) 4. Optimism.
5. Self-management (Psychology) I. Selby, John, 1945- II. Title.
  HF5386.H2455 2006
  650.1--dc22

2006001665
ISBN 1-57174-467-3

10 9 8 7 6 5 4 3 2
Printed on acid-free paper in China

It is not enough to have a good mind.
The main thing is to use it well.
- René Descartes

TAKING CHARGE

You have an amazing power available to you, anywhere and anytime. This is the power to take charge of your mind. You possess the power to make yourself happy or sad; the power to change your thoughts and emotions or run on automatic pilot; and the power to move to an upbeat, energetic mood or sink into lethargy. This is a power that everyone enjoys. It does not depend on your status, your wealth, or your circumstances in life. Instead it depends on where you choose to focus your attention moment to moment.

You have always had this power, yet you probably seldom use it. Now you can learn to how to turn your power on and take charge of your mind, whenever and wherever you want. All you need to do is follow our simple method and break free of the cycle of negative, unconscious habits that tend to toss us around like a rudderless ship in a stormy ocean.

Do you currently feel that you have almost no control over what mood, energy level, or mental shape you wake up in each day? On rare lucky days you might wake up in super-charge gear – your overall attitude positive and your thoughts razor-sharp. You radiate charisma, you're brimming with new ideas, your body feels good – there's just no stopping you.

But on far too many days, as you well know, you tend to wake up with your energy level low and your mind dull, your emotions depressed or anxious and your body sluggish. When you show up at work feeling this way, the results can be mediocre or even disastrous. But rather than feeling in charge of your mind and able to shift into a brighter experience, you feel like a helpless victim of unknown forces that drag you down and leave you flat.

It's time to discover how to shift from feeling like a victim of your mood swings to being in charge of your mind and emotions. The key question is this: What factors at work are beyond your ability to control, and what factors can you, in fact, take charge of and change to your benefit?

You know all the external factors at work that you don't have control over. Your job is almost certainly defined, with few opportunities for alteration. If you could change your external situation at work, you already would have.

But there remains the most important factor of all: the moment-to-moment choice of where you aim your mind's extraordinary power of attention – which, in turn, determines for each new moment what you focus on and experience, how strong and flexible you feel mentally, how you respond to your coworkers, and what you achieve at work.

The act of taking charge of your mind will enable you to manage your emotional mood and mental performance. You can attain this inner goal without relying on a new culture, new management, or new organization. On your own, you can get in mental and emotional shape, and make a profound, permanent change in your life.

To gain and maintain optimum mental strength and clarity at work, you'll find that you can employ our methods quickly and unobtrusively, right in the heat of a busy workday. No one will know what you're doing inside your mind, but they'll notice that suddenly your mood brightens, you flash with great ideas, and you're a pleasure to spend time with.

Why are you able to accomplish so much so fast? Because, in our method, as you shift your mind's attention away from internal stressors that are dragging you down, you also turn your mind's attention toward thoughts and experiences that immediately lift you up. You flex your mental and emotional power!

INSTANT ACCESS ⇌ FAST HELP

CONTENTS

CORE SKILLS FOR SUCCESS

Do you want to earn a higher salary? Do you want to be promoted or run your own business? Do you want to enjoy yourself more at work and reduce your level of stress? Do you want to make more friends in the office, build strong customer relationships, and be part of a high-performance team? Do you want to achieve a healthy balance between work and home?

If you want to achieve these goals, you have chosen the right book, for in the following pages you will learn a powerful new method to improve both your performance at work *and* your job satisfaction. The great news is that you can do both, not one at the expense of the other.

It's often assumed that success is based on attending the best business school, working for the market leader, or having the highest IQ. But there are many thousands of brilliant, highly qualified people who achieve little. And there are also many apparently successful people who are unhappy and lack meaning in their lives. There are likewise millions of people who struggle every day to stay focused, energetic, motivated, and passionate. All of us want to be successful and happy at work. The problem is we either don't know how to get there, or we use the wrong strategies, trying to change the world around us rather than taking charge of our own minds.

The real action at work is not going on around you, but inside you. Learning to manage your own mind is the key to unlocking your potential at work, achieving extraordinary results, and enjoying extraordinary levels of happiness. We will help you apply the mind-management key so that you activate inherent mental and emotional powers that you have had all along.

The most qualified people can be held back by mental and emotional habits which they seem powerless to change – because it is the quality of your thinking and the brightness of your moods that determine your success, more than any other factors. And this quality of mind is not just about IQ or even emotional intelligence. It is about effectively taking charge of the amazing power of your mind.

Just as with physical fitness, everyone can actively enhance their mental powers and improve their performance results by learning the mind-management tools in our book. Fortunately, the tools are simple and easy to use. There are no big, difficult ideas here. The science behind them might be complex – what we have done is distil the psychological essence and create a method which is both easy to apply and genuinely transformative.

Imagine a career of consistently making the right decisions; of being focused rather than distracted, calm rather than restless, powerful rather than dull and listless. Imagine a lifetime of being in a positive mood rather than a negative one; of being confident rather than anxious; of helping others rather than being self-absorbed.

The programs in this book will enable you to achieve the above goals. Our methods work. We know they work because of their grounding in psychology, business practices, and, above all, from our own direct experience. The vast majority of business and self-help books have good ideas. The problem is that they remain just that – ideas. Our intention is to get you beyond the idea to where you are actively employing our Take Charge techniques at work – so you can see for yourself how well they get the job done.

The logic is clear. If you want to take charge of your career, your happiness, and the quality of your life, first you must learn to manage your mind. You do not need to spend years in college learning psychology or years in India learning meditation. You just need to learn a short daily exercise routine, so that you get strong and fit in your mind and emotions, like you would with a physical fitness routine.

We welcome you to relax and embark with us on the most exciting journey of all – the journey of discovering your own remarkable inner powers. Take charge of your mind, get strong and creative in your thoughts and healthy and happy in your emotions. Take the challenge – your entire life will change when you do.

Whatever type of work you are doing and whatever type of organization you work for, this book will help you achieve greater success – and at the same time increase your sense of enjoyment and well-being both at work and at home. When you make the decision to take charge of your own mind, you'll find that you gain tremendous power – the power to overcome negative thoughts, moods, and anxieties; the power to maintain focus, creativity, and insight; and the power to be a superb communicator and charismatic leader.

In organizations everywhere, employees and managers alike

are feeling more and more vulnerable and stressed on the job. Unpredictable changes, hypercompetition, outsourcing, downsizing, long hours, and technological overload threaten to overwhelm even the most stalwart employee. By implementing our new Take Charge method, you'll gain control of your own success, rather than remaining at the mercy of all the turbulent changes transforming the world of work.

You spend at least half your waking hours at work. If you don't learn to manage your own mind and moods, the non-stop tensions and uncertainties will tend to knock you down, impairing your physical and mental health and triggering stress-related deterioration in work performance.

The time has come, as you read this new book, to discover that you don't have to be a victim to pressures at work. You can take charge, become master of your own ship, and actively create harmony and increased prosperity for yourself – and for your organization as well.

The truth is, you probably cannot change the world of work – but you can most definitely change how you feel and how you perform at work.

Specifically, you can decide to improve your own interior experience at work, learn to take charge of your own mind – and transform the way you respond to and overcome the pressures and demands of work. Our Take Charge mind-management program will help you accomplish this major goal.

PRIMARY SKILLS

The vast majority of books on performance, management, and leadership focus on techniques for managing others and trying to change them. This book does just the opposite. It gives you the strategies needed to manage your own mind more effectively – which is the most important step to managing yourself, your career, and other people.

You've probably read numerous business articles and books and attended training courses, and in the process acquired general knowledge about many tools and techniques. But how much of that training was truly helpful in the long run – are you still using those tools at work?

The Take Charge method offers many advantages over other approaches to achieving increased performance and happiness at work.

First and foremost, it is *practical.* We have distilled a number of leading, complex concepts from the fields of psychology, stress management, and organizational behavior into simple techniques which anyone can remember to use. Our only goal is to provide a simple, easy-to-use guide for everyone at work.

Second, it is *relevant.* The Take Charge method has been developed to solve the most urgent problems that people face at work. Our method helps you deal with stress, low energy, distraction, fear, anxiety, and mood swings. These feelings represent a chronic problem in the workplace, and prevent millions of employees from reaching their full potential.

Third, the benefits of our method are *immediate.* You don't need years of practice or extra qualifications to reap the benefits of using our method. When you practice the simple techniques, you will notice immediate improvements which can transform your daily experience at work today!

Fourth, our method is *integrated.* We have incorporated what we believe are the most important skills needed for you to take charge of your mind and boost your performance. These include confidence, self-esteem, empathy, creativity, and wisdom. Each step of our process builds on the others and provides a powerful, integrated system of change.

Finally, our method is *effective.* If you follow the steps in the following pages you will notice real improvements. You will feel more calm, more centered, and more focused. You will notice that you are more productive, make better decisions, and build stronger relationships.

> To apply new knowledge and skills successfully, you need to consciously manage your focus of attention. Only then can you practice and apply new ideas and tools in your work routine.

Everyone wants to become more creative, more resilient, and more flexible. We all want to be great at "execution" and strategic thinking. Yet what underlies these skills and techniques? What do we have to do moment to moment in our minds to attain mastery of the latest breakthrough business strategies? In our book you will learn how to build the foundation for these strategies by taking charge of your thinking, your moods, and your emotions.

For example, all organizations want someone who is great at execution or simply "getting things done." The basis for this is being highly focused in the present moment and having the self-discipline to complete the job. This involves being in control of your thinking and concentrating on the task, not on negative feelings, fears, or anxieties associated with the task. We will show how to do this and how to distinguish yourself from the majority of employees who struggle with difficulty to stay on track and execute effectively.

This book will show you how to master the most effective new cognitive tools. These tools are simple yet powerful strategies that will boost your performance and improve your results at work.

COGNITIVE SHIFTING

You don't need to struggle with complex concepts or go back to school to master our new method. We've distilled decades of research in business management, organizational behavior, communication skills, stress control, and creativity enhancement into two simple yet potent methods based on the psychological process of "cognitive shifting."

> "Cognitive shifting" is the ability to move
> readily between different states of mind
> in order to optimize mental performance.

By exploring our Wake Up and Take Charge methods, you'll discover the extraordinary power of this new cognitive-shifting process. You can instantly shift into the optimum state of mind for each challenge you face at work. It's like having a remote control for your brain – you can shift to optimum moods and mental states whenever you want.

Our Take Charge method includes a unique set of short Focus Phrases that (after brief training) will instantly stimulate the full cognitive shift you need at the moment. In the process, you'll gain effective control over your thoughts and moods leading to a peak mindset and superior performance.

You'll find that you can make these shifts, and reap the benefits, in just one Wake Up minute if that's all the time you have for a super-quick upswing. Plus at least several times a day, you'll want to spend a few dedicated minutes employing our full Take Charge method for tapping deeper at-work creative and leadership skills. We also offer a potent at-home self-advancement version of this process, to further enhance your power to run your mind at full throttle. Indeed the more you practice our method the more you accumulate the benefits of being in your peak mindset. Soon this higher state becomes habitual and you move to a whole new level of extraordinary clarity, insight, and mastery.

SEVEN PRIMARY STEPS

In a very brief outline, here are our seven primary cognitive-shifting steps. As you'll discover, each step builds on the previous ones as you move through the full process. This daily "mental work-out" method has been specifically developed to provide a solution for the most urgent needs at work – to stay in the present moment, manage your mood swings, develop more empathy for customer bonding, be more creative and charismatic – and make wiser decisions. This is a fast yet powerful daily exercise routine for the mind, integrating a wide range of vital skills via seven special focus phrases. Serving as your building blocks for high-level performance, these focus phrases are the distillation of long-term research based on advanced theories of consciousness management.

The focus phrases are easy to remember and easy to use. Each one triggers powerful thoughts and emotions which immediately improve your mood, and take you towards a peak state of mind. This enables you to gain the benefits from the best practices in the fields of psychology, organizational behavior, and meditation without having to read hundreds of books and studies.

It has taken us many decades of research and practice to refine these practices into an easy-to-use, relevant, and effective process for improving your levels of performance and happiness at work. We have deliberately excluded scientific references and any other information which detract from the simplicity and power of our method. For those readers who want to know about the scientific background to our method, we have put a summary of the relevant research, evidence, and related readings for each chapter at the end of the book.

STEP ONE: Be More Alert ~ Feel Better

Core Need: "I want to learn to focus my attention intently on my work, build more energy, manage change effectively, and feel more healthy."

Our Solution: With our method, you can quickly shift from being distracted, dull, and lost in thought to feeling fully present, alert, and responsive - while also enjoying the present moment.

STEP TWO: Stop Worrying ~ Feel More Confident

Core Need: "I want to let go of worries, feel positive, handle stress and anxiety better, and keep my mood calm and confident."

Our Solution: This second step enables you to put aside anxious thoughts so that you feel more grounded, positive, and healthy - radiating confidence and clarity through managing your moods more effectively.

STEP THREE: COMMUNICATE WITH EMPATHY

Core Need: "I want to feel accepted and emotionally engaged at work, building warm productive relationships with colleagues and customers."

Our Solution: The Take Charge process shifts your attention toward positive emotions that spread trust, cooperation, and respect. You will enhance your emotional intelligence and network at higher levels.

STEP FOUR: BOOST YOUR SELF-ESTEEM

Core Need: "I want to be optimistic, enjoy a positive self-image, and be more charismatic."

Our Solution: This fourth step of our method quiets self-criticism and feelings of inadequacy, so you can wholeheartedly accept yourself and enhance your popularity and leadership.

STEP FIVE: SOLVE PROBLEMS MORE CREATIVELY

Core Need: "I want to be more creative and innovative in developing new ideas and solving problems."

Our Solution: This fifth step shifts your focus of attention beyond conventional uninspired thinking and humdrum solutions, by integrating all five of your mind's intelligence sources.

STEP SIX: TAP YOUR VISIONARY WISDOM

Core Need: "I want to think strategically, see the whole picture, and make wise decisions."

Our Solution: This vital sixth step shifts you from being stuck in cleverness and short-term thinking toward making contact with your deeper perspective – and generating intuitive vision.

STEP SEVEN: ACT WITH INTEGRITY

Core Need: "I want to take and implement the right decisions, not the easy ones."

Our Solution: This final Take Charge step enables you to state your underlying purpose and then act with courage and integrity.

"FULL-MIND WORKOUT"
MENTAL FITNESS PROGRAM

Once you practice and master the basic Take Charge method you can also use the process as a daily mental/emotional workout routine. Just like you need a regular routine of physical exercise to stay healthy, fit, and attractive, you also need a daily mental and emotional workout program to stay fit and sharp. In just five minutes a day you can move through a complete mental exercise routine that will not only strengthen your three primary "mental muscle groups" but also make you feel better and more powerful.

Each day of the week at work, we'll teach you how to quickly move through the seven-step Take Charge process so that you exercise all your mental and emotional muscles. Then for that particular day you'll do additional mental exercises to strengthen that day's mental focus.

Yes, superior cognitive power and emotional well-being do require a bit of disciplined daily exercise, just like with your physical body. But the results are immediate and positive – our Full-Mind Workout program will make you feel better each day and, at the same time, strengthen your ability to maintain high awareness, genuine empathy, exceptional creativity – and a strong sense of charisma.

It will take you a few weeks of daily exercise to get in shape at deeper consciousness levels – and it will take regular repetition to maintain and increase your mental prowess. But just like with regular physical exercise, once you discover just how good mental and emotional workouts make you feel, you'll never want to stop! Our weekly schedule will serve as a lifelong mental-fitness program because each week you'll keep getting more and more fit at mental and emotional levels that really count. To help you to effortlessly establish a daily Full-Mind Workout, we also offer online audio guidance to move you through each day's exercise routine.

FIVE MODES OF CONSCIOUSNESS

What are the primary "mental muscles" that you can learn to exercise and develop to your advantage? Let's look scientifically at the inner-focus choices available to you at any given moment, which you can take charge of and strengthen. Please note that although this discussion is purposefully not over-heavy in scientific explanation, all scientific discussions and research are described and documented at the end of this book.

Beyond basic biological operations, your mind has five quite distinct "mental muscle groups" – separate functions of the brain that have evolved over the last million years into an amazing instrument of consciousness. Each moment, once you take charge, you have the power to choose which function or mixture of functions to flex and employ, and which to temporarily allow to relax.

Much of your business success depends on being in the right mode of consciousness at the right time and place. Soon MBA classes will be teaching all this – but until now we've been stuck in the dark ages when it comes to this higher-order knowledge and skill. It's time to get clear on our five "mental muscle groups" and start getting them in better shape.

Again: The act of cognitive shifting is the process through which you shift from one mental mode to another and focus on strengthening a particular mental or emotional power. Here's a short description of each of the five modes of mental functioning that you possess in your mind:

1. Sensory Perception: You possess the power of whole-body sensory awareness (seeing, smelling, touching, hearing, tasting), which exists entirely in the present moment in your physical body. This mental power enables you to receive direct sensory information (experience) from the world around you and to be aware of your physical and emotional presence. At work, this present-moment sensory world is where all the action takes place. It is the root of self-awareness and awareness of others, and essential for present-moment attention and effective action. To keep this "mental muscle group" exercised and healthy is essential.

2. Conceptual Thought: You also possess a remarkable deductive-thinking power, through which you reflect on perceptual experiences and actively generate beliefs and concepts, plans and assessments. Most of the time, you're probably caught in this valuable past-future mode – it gets exercised a great deal at work. Conceptual thinking is essential for activities such as strategy, brainstorming, and planning. But left uncontrolled it can also overpower your sensory performance and your ability to respond to what is happening right now in front of you. It is a dominant mental power which you need to manage or else it will take over and manage you.

3. Emotional Experience: Thirdly, you have the power to feel an emotional response to your experiences and thoughts. Your emotions, such as fear, anger, joy, depression, and contentment, are experienced physically in your body in the present moment. They are a response to thoughts and memories and imaginings, as well as to present-moment experience. In a feedback loop, emotions then augment or interfere with the thinking process and your physical well-being. We will show you how to recognize the subtle connection between thinking and emotions, and how to strengthen positive and supportive emotions at work. Especially in sales and service, keeping your empathy muscle strong and healthy is essential to success.

4. Memory/Imagination: You also have a powerful mental function that remembers events from the past and imagines possible events happening in the future. You need to strengthen and fine-tune, and also discipline, this mental muscle. Left to their own devices, your memory and imagination can recall many negative experiences and generate anxiety and energy loss. We'll teach you how to take charge of these powerful mental processes and ensure that they work for you rather than against you. Then you can selectively access valuable memories and experiences, and use your imagination for setting goals and creating a vision.

5. Intuition/Wisdom: Finally, we come to the intuitive-insight power of the mind. Your entire brain and nervous system has the capacity to light up at once with instant flashes of realization and knowing. By perceiving the whole of a situation, this higher integrative power of your mind has the strength to generate wise decisions and a sense of inner certainty and vision, which are essential to success at work. We will teach you how to shift away from habitual thought and flex your insight muscle, so you can see patterns, gain insight, and make connections not available in routine thought.

So there you have your mind in a nutshell – the basic ingredients that make up your moment-to-moment experience and power at work. These five "mental muscle groups" represent the entire potential of your personal awareness. The cognitive-shifting method taught in this book will enable you to flex whichever mode of consciousness best suits your situation at any given moment.

FIVE-STAR INTEGRATION

There are times when you employ just one of these awareness modes. Perhaps you're focused perceptually while driving in difficult traffic – or you're busy thinking through figures at work. Most of the time, however, your mind employs two or three of its five functions at the same time, to generate the experience of any given moment. There exist many variations to the basic awareness theme.

> The trick to successful consciousness management
> is knowing how to relax and shift away from
> particular mental tensions and fixations, so that you
> break free from bothersome emotions or thoughts
> or memories – and then redirect your mind's
> power of attention in more positive directions.

For instance, it's important at work to shift regularly out of past-future thinking into sensory-perception mode – because this present-moment perceptual level of your mind's awareness is where you encounter all new information at work and where day-to-day business actually takes place. All communication is also a sensory event; decisions are made in the present moment; sales happen in the here-and-now – this perceptual dimension of consciousness is the powerhouse that generates excellent performance.

There are also many times a day when you need to shift from "experiencing" to "reflecting" about your business situation, as you process information into conceptual formats and think deductively about your situation. The emotional function of your mind is also vital at work, because so much of success is dependent on how you feel, how you relate to others, and how well you manage your moods at work. Employing memory and imagination is also effective at work. Most of your pragmatic thinking involves the raw ingredients of memories and then the resulting future-projections. Problem-solving is all about evaluating memories and imagining alternative futures. Finally, the intuitive-creative function of the mind is also essential – for flashes of insight and vision and for becoming more grounded in your deeper sense of integrity at work.

Clearly, you do best by keeping all five of these "mental muscle groups" exercised and healthy. We call this "five-star integration" – gaining the power and finesse to employ your mind's total power in the most appropriate way, each moment of the day.

WHO BENEFITS MOST?

Most human-resource programs are divided into two quite different segments: one for top management, the other for everyone else. Our Take Charge methods don't have this division because they benefit everyone equally. There is no job high or low in a company that won't be improved by applying our two methods regularly. Each member of an organization is crucial to the success of that organization. The quality of inner experience that each person maintains determines, without question, the overall quality of consciousness (and success) of the whole organization.

Our intent is to provide an entire organization with these basic mind-management tools, so that the organization as a whole benefits. What is the impact of everyone learning to take charge of their minds at work? First of all, the general atmosphere of the organization becomes less stressed and tense, and more relaxed and enjoyable. There is greater cooperation and genuine team spirit. As everyone learns to stay more aware and alert, productivity increases and results improve. In this high-performance culture, creativity and insight are enhanced, better decisions are made, and teamwork flourishes.

Of equal importance, the physical and emotional well-being of the whole organization steadily increases: Medical and insurance costs drop significantly, fewer days are lost to absenteeism, and worker morale rises and remains high.

Above all, you will be able to attract and retain talented employees, because the best people want to work for organizations where there is a high-energy, vibrant, and positive culture. Creating this buzz of vitality and excitement in the workplace may be even more important than providing the highest salaries or the best promotion prospects. It will certainly give your organization a vital edge in the competition for talent.

So whether you're a senior executive or junior secretary, president or trainee manager – whatever your position, the skills you learn in this book will not only help you personally toward success and fulfillment, they will help your organization become more compassionate, positive, creative, and successful.

TAKE CHARGE LEARNING CURVE

Even though the payoff is dramatic, you'll find that mastering the Wake Up and Take Charge methods isn't difficult. You'll learn the techniques in a couple of weeks, devoting just ten to 15 minutes a day to training – and in a month, you'll have fully integrated the program into your work life.

You'll find that, right from the initial week, you'll be able to apply what you're learning and feel the benefits at work. And as the weeks and months go by and you get better at the process, the more you'll notice an improvement in your daily business experience.

You probably have your own preferred ways for learning something new. The following suggestions are general recommendations on how best to master these new at-work techniques. Feel free to finesse the plan to make it your own.

Phase One: Take in the Whole . . . When beginning to learn something new, it's best to obtain first an overview of the program, to "see the whole" of the process. Therefore, we recommend that you first read through this entire book fairly rapidly, fast enough to get a taste for the entire process. Enjoy the read!

Phase Two: Mastering the Method . . . We recommend that you then set aside two weeks, go back to the first chapter, and devote at least one full day to each of the ten chapters. Read the chapter once again – and practice the short process taught in that chapter over and over. Throughout that day at work, say the

Focus Phrase you're learning many times to yourself in different work situations, to point your mind's attention toward the cognitive-shifting experience you're mastering.

Phase Three: Application Strategy . . . Once you've memorized all the Focus Phrases and explored the inner shifting process each initiates, you're ready to begin selectively applying your cognitive tools. In each chapter, and especially in chapter 9, we give you specific at-work suggestions and assignments, so that you have ample guidance throughout this learning process. You'll want to employ the daily Full-Mind Workout, plus the specific applications offered in the book.

Phase Four: Long-term Success . . . After you've moved through the full training program, you're free to use these Take Charge consciousness-management tools to your advantage whenever and however you choose. For the rest of your life, these primary techniques will continue to keep you mentally and emotionally fit, and take you deeper into discovering and applying your higher potential at work.

You'll also find that your life outside work
begins to noticeably improve, as you relate
more successfully to your family and friends.

In chapter 10 (and also online at http://takechargetraining.com), you'll find important at-home programs for expanding the Take Charge process into a daily reflection practice and health-enhancement support system – to help you move further into tapping your ultimate potential as the days and years go by. Our aim is to offer a total at-work performance and wellness program for you and your family.

ONLINE AND AUDIO SUPPORT

http://takechargetraining.com

We've designed this guidebook to be enjoyable and effective in and of itself. You don't need any other inputs in order to master these programs. At the same time, many people also benefit from an audio dimension to their learning experience. For those of you wanting audio support and guidance, we've fully backed up the written learning process with online audio-training sessions and other support systems. Please take advantage of the online training, community, and long-term support you'll find at http://takechargetraining.com. There are also MP3 downloads and CD versions of the training programs so you can practice with audio guidance away from your computer, plus in-house and online corporate programs. This unique friendly site is designed as a complete support system, augmenting our written discussion with ongoing forums and trainer updates to keep you fresh and challenged as you continue to explore the fine art of managing your mind to your advantage.

And so – the zone awaits. Enjoy the next few weeks as you master the Wake Up and Take Charge methods. The learning curve is steep – and you'll enjoy each step of the way. Furthermore there's no end to how far you can advance in this process. The potential of your mind is vast . . . and awaits your discovery.

PART ONE

"Wake Up" Alertness Program

Be master of mind
rather than
mastered by mind.
- Zen proverb

CHAPTER 1

PRESENT-MOMENT EMPOWERMENT

CHAPTER ONE: PREVIEW

Core Need – Sharpen Your Focus: With so many pressures on your time and attention, it's essential to master skills that enable you to stay focused, sharp, and energetic at work. You need to know how to let go immediately of inner distractions that inhibit your ability to complete projects on time. When all's said and done, employees who maintain a high level of energy, who pay attention to the task at hand, and who concentrate the most effectively will be the most successful.

Our Solution: Using our short-form Wake Up process, in just one minute, you can shift out of distracting mental and emotional fixations into a more energetic, effective, enjoyable state of mind, where you're fully engaged and mentally alert.

The Process: In each new moment, your quality of work is determined by where you choose to focus your power of attention. Using the Wake Up process, you can shift your mind's attention toward four primary physical focus points that, in turn, wake you up to the present moment, make you feel better, and brighten both your mood and your performance.

Your Payoff: This unique "be sharp" cognitive-shifting skill will boost your success at work as you become more powerful, creative, healthy, and charismatic in the present moment. This Wake Up tool will also serve as your foundation for moving through the full Take Charge method.

DILEMMA AT WORK

Larry is vice president of business development for a successful manufacturing company in New England. At first glance, he's perfectly qualified for his job. He is smart and has an MBA from a leading business school. But he faces a major challenge: He is regularly sabotaging his own performance through his inability to control his mind and stay focused. All too often, when he needs to focus tightly on what he's doing in the present moment, his attention shifts to remembering something that happened the night before, or ahead to imagining something in the future. He's plagued with the universal habit of attention loss – and his career is suffering as a result as he drifts from one uncompleted project to another.

The solution to Larry's problem at work is for him to learn how to take charge of his own mind – and regularly shift his attention back to the present moment where all the interaction at work actually takes place. He needs to master the Wake Up method for regaining the present moment, so that every time he begins to lose focus on the task at hand, he can instantly shift his attention to be fully alert and engaged in his work.

At the core of Larry's consciousness, and everybody else's, there's a primary act that we are doing all the time, that determines absolutely everything else that happens in our life. Where we focus our attention is where our creative energy and our power to take action naturally flow.

> Therefore absolutely everything in our life depends on where we choose to focus our almighty power of attention, moment to moment. This choice is your real power.

Most people most of the time aren't assuming conscious responsibility for where they are aiming their mind's attention. Instead, they're letting ingrained habits or outside influences determine where they consume their precious resource. Taking charge of your mind means waking up to the present moment, becoming aware of where you're directing your power of attention, and then making new choices regarding where to direct that inner power.

> You possess an amazing power – and where you focus that power ultimately determines what you achieve. To see this clearly and act on it is probably the greatest step forward you can take in your life.

Right now, notice what you are choosing to focus on – for instance, what sensory inputs are you tuned into? You are, of course, aware of the words you're reading right now on this page, and perhaps the weight of this book. Perhaps you're also aware of sounds around you, and vaguely the space of the room you're in. And you're somewhat aware of your own body . . .

You're also probably aware that there's an underlying thought in your mind that is maintaining your focus on this book by saying to you, "Let's continue reading this book because it's interesting and might prove useful." If another thought came through your mind related to an interest in another direction, your focus of attention would probably follow that thought, and you'd shift your focus elsewhere, right?

THOUGHTS DETERMINE EVERYTHING

Research in cognitive psychology has shown that our thoughts determine the quality of our emotions, moods, actions, and life-experience. So nothing is more urgent or more important than learning how to take charge of our thinking. If you observe your own mind, you'll find that it's true. Except in the case of totally reflexive actions, before you do anything, there will appear a thought in your mind that provokes that action.

These thoughts are mostly subliminal, an ingrained habit – but if you watch yourself moment to moment, you'll find that the scientists are right: Your thoughts ultimately do direct your action. They are also what stimulates most of your emotions.

Even though it's now proven that our behavior is a result of our thoughts and ingrained habits, most of the time most people have no control over the thoughts that run through their minds and provoke their moods and activities. That's why most people feel like victims of their mood swings and negative mind states.

It is almost impossible to stop thoughts from arising – the key is to take charge of them. What we're exploring here is your power to shift away from all your negative thought-flows and consciously begin to hold thoughts in your mind that refocus your attention in productive and enjoyable ways. Taking charge of your own thoughts is so important – and yet it's quite easy to do once you see the psychological logic and take the time to learn our set of cognitive-shifting tools (Focus Phrases) that help redirect your power of attention where you want it to go.

CHOOSE YOUR STATE OF MIND

As you know from your own inner experience, you are always in one mind state or another. You are busily focusing on certain thoughts, memories, imaginations, or external events – and your emotions and physical condition are being affected by whatever you're focusing on.

You, of course, have a wide variety of possible states of mind, each one involving a particular combination of thoughts, perceptions, memories, and imaginings. For example, your angry mind states are probably generated when you fixate on a present conflict or dwell on an unresolved past conflict. Your hostile thoughts and memories, in turn, make your body respond with aggressive tensions as your heartbeat increases and your breathing tightens – you know this pattern?

If you want to shift out of this angry mood, what can you do? Well – if your anger is being stimulated by a present-moment threat, obviously you need to deal with that threat. But otherwise, you must take charge of your thoughts, shift away from the memories and associations that are provoking the angry emotion, and turn your attention in more productive, positive directions. Otherwise, especially at work, staying stuck in such a negative mood is going to damage your success as well as your health.

The following is a short list of mind states that we all experience in our workdays. The fine art of cognitive shifting involves learning how to shift your mind's attention rapidly from the negative states toward more positive ones you want to highlight at work:

Negative States	Positive States
mentally foggy	fully aware
worried	confident
rejecting	accepting
unfriendly	empathic
narrow-minded	creative
weak	strong
distracted	focused
disturbed	peaceful
confused	certain
stressed	healthy
manipulative	participatory
depressed	happy
angry	friendly
foolish	wise

Being able to shift from negative to positive mind states might, at first, seem very difficult – and until recently, this was true. But recent breakthroughs in our understanding of the cognitive-shifting process have generated shortcuts in the shifting process, so that you can readily master new mental tools that enable you to take charge of your mind without any training in psychology.

You don't need to grasp the internal operations of your car's engine in order to jump in and roar down the road, and you don't have to grasp fully the scientific explanations of how your mind works in order to shift into more fulfilling states of mind.

WAKE UP STRATEGY

Whatever your particular type of work, you've been hired with the clear understanding that you will stay focused on the present moment, so that you maintain a consistently high level of alertness and concentration on the job. Successful organizations need their employees to remain focused on the work at hand, rather than drifting off and away.

Communication, by its very nature, happens right here and now. The people who best hold their full attention in the here and now tend to be the best listeners and the best communicators on the team. And when you're alone, the more often you return your attention to the present moment and wake up to your senses, the better you'll do at work. Not only will you be a better communicator – you'll also be more efficient at gathering new relevant information because, by its very nature, new information always emerges into view in the present moment.

Of course, as mentioned earlier, at work, you often need to shift your mind's attention away from the present moment, into cognitive thinking and problem-solving. To be temporarily lost in thought is essential for reflecting on past experience and planning for future action. But you can't be entirely lost in thought and at the same time be aware of what's happening in the present moment. It's a choice you're always making – to be lost in thought, or open to new information and experience.

That's why, in mind management, the term "cognitive shifting" is so important – because over and over during a hectic workday, you need to shift quickly and smoothly from intense problem-solving and reflective thought, back into present-moment engagement with other people and your work environment. How exactly is this mental shifting accomplished?

THE WAKE UP PROCESS

Imagine that you're at work, and realize that you've let yourself become caught up in a less-than-optimum mood and mind state. Your mental clarity is low, you feel distracted – you woke up on the wrong side of the bed, you're worrying about one thing after another even while trying to get your job done. Maybe your boss hollered at you for no reason at all – and regardless of the cause, you're off-center.

Having realized the relatively low place you're in, you now need to do something specific that will shift your inner experience away from the thoughts, memories, and imaginings that are provoking your low state of mind, and take charge of your situation by reestablishing a cool, calm composure in the present moment. You need, in a word, to regain your senses.

WAKE UP Step One: We've found that the most powerful

action you can take to instantly shift your focus of attention into the present moment is to say to yourself, "I feel the air flowing in and out of my nose," and allow these words to turn your attention to exactly what you've pointed toward – the actual sensation happening as you breathe . . . the feel of the air flowing in and the air flowing out of your nose.

> The immediate physical sensation of the air flowing in and out of your nose, like a jolt from another dimension, instantly shifts your awareness away from past-future fixations and emotions, toward the powerful wake up impact of your own vital presence here and now.

Especially on your inhalations, you'll feel the sensation of the air flowing through your nose, and this core perception will override your thoughts about the past and the future as you choose to shift into your experience in the present moment.

The beauty of our method is that you can change your awareness of your breath easily and instantly and, when you do, this triggers positive changes in your thinking and then in your mood. Breathing is the key that unlocks the door to improved states of consciousness and performance.

We'll spend considerable time throughout this training program making sure you master this quite remarkable focus of attention. The only tool you need to memorize to shift your focus of attention to this first Wake Up step is to say to yourself, "I feel the air flowing in and out of my nose," and let the words activate this experience.

WAKE UP Step Two: The second step expands your awareness in the present moment into full three-dimensional alertness by including not only your nose and head, but also your chest and belly in your awareness of your breathing experience.

Just say, "I'm also aware of the movements in my chest and belly," and your awareness will expand to include the volume and movement of your body as you breathe.

As we'll explore in depth later, this seemingly simple act of expanding your awareness to include the immediate sensory experience of your nose, your head, and also your chest and belly has the psychological power to quiet all thoughts instantly – providing instant relief from the two-dimensional world of distracting thoughts as you pop back into the three-dimensional world of sensory experience. In other words you stop being "in your head," lost in conceptual thought, and move out to being in your body as a whole – fully aware and responsive in the present moment.

This shift in mental focus dissolves worried and angry thoughts because, as cognitive science has demonstrated, we can't focus on thoughts about the past and the future and at the same time experience two or more sensations in the body in the present moment.

Learning this cognitive shift will only require
a few weeks of practice, and you will
quickly notice how much better you feel!

There are strong lifelong habits to overcome here, and the only way to establish new habits is to discipline yourself and move through the process enough times so that the power of the procedure begins to have effect.

For the first ten to 20 times of walking yourself through the process, you're still in beginner's/learning mode, and you'll need to be a little patient – until suddenly you reach that promised point where it happens, you pop fully into the present moment and come alive in the here and now.

WAKE UP Step Three: The first two steps of the Wake Up process shift your attention to the present-moment happening of your own breathing. You can move quite quickly through these first two steps, in just two to four breaths. If your organization has offered generic meditation training for reducing stress and improving energy and well-being, you might have learned a similar breath meditation.

But what we've found in our Wake Up research is that most people, when told to focus just on their breathing, quickly slip back into thinking – and end up feeling rather frustrated. The solution is to expand your awareness fairly quickly to include another vital dimension of your ongoing present moment – the emotional feelings in your heart.

While continuing to stay aware of your breathing experience, say to yourself the clear statement of intent that will wake you up to the world of emotions and compassion: "I'm also aware of the feelings in my heart."

The feelings you are holding in your heart at any given moment represent the core emotional mood dominating your personal presence at work. If you want to shift from being neutral or moody, detached, and bored at work to radiating empathy and good feelings, this third step of consciously focusing your mind's attention toward the feelings in your heart will prove not only powerful, but absolutely essential to do – and do often.

Most people find that when they first tune in to the feelings in their hearts, there's not much feeling there at all. It's important to note that often at work, you're mostly numb in your heart – feeling hardly anything at all. And the feelings you do sometimes encounter in your heart at work tend to be those of anger, frustration, apprehension, and so forth, not good feelings.

This is clearly counterproductive because your emotions impact those around you. If you are not acting from your heart, you run the risk of appearing cold, distant, and unfeeling. Your success at work depends on generating the opposite feelings. It depends on acting from your heart to radiate warmth, openness, and sincerity.

So it's definitely wise to deal with whatever numb or negative feelings you find when you say, "I'm aware of the feelings in my heart." Cognitive studies have documented that just through the act of regularly pausing and turning your mind's attention to your heart, you stimulate a sense of relaxation, expansion, warmth, and the inflow of good feelings into your heart.

NOTE: When your heart feels temporarily overwhelmed with angry, cold, or fearful emotions, you can actively encourage the inflow of positive feelings into your heart by recalling the love you feel for someone in your life – perhaps a spouse or other family member, a lover or close friend – or a favorite song, landscape, and so on. As you feel warmth, acceptance, and love in your heart for that person, place, or whatever, you'll find that your breathing deepens and you come more alive and human in the present moment.

WAKE UP Step Four: In less than one minute, once you master this primary cognitive-shifting process, you'll be able to accomplish a great deal – you'll wake up to your physical presence, quiet distracting thoughts and worries, relax and deepen your breathing – and become grounded in good feelings in your heart.

At this point, you're just one step away from totally regaining your sense of well-being and empowerment in the present moment.

You now need to say to yourself the fourth and final step in the Wake Up process, which takes you into total full-body awareness and empowerment: "I'm aware of my whole body at once, here in this present moment."

This shift into whole-body awareness is something you naturally experience many times a day. When you pause and enjoy a moment of peace and beauty on the way to work or a moment in a delicious meal, when you go jogging, play golf, or watch a beautiful sunset – these are moments when you are totally focused in the here and now. Many movements and perceptions naturally snap your awareness into "the zone" so that you experience the whole at once.

What you're learning in this method is how to shift at will into this expansive "in the zone" feeling of being totally present in your body. This whole-body feeling, as you'll discover for yourself step by step, is the root quality of charisma, of empathy, of enjoyment. People who are present in their whole bodies at work have that special, radiant presence that other people respond to – and now you can regain this powerful, grounded posture at work, whenever you want to.

> The experience of popping suddenly out
> of negative emotions and bothersome thoughts
> into the bright fresh air of the present moment is
> one of the most liberating experiences possible.

You always have the choice, the power, and the ability to manage your mind to accomplish this inner shifting experience. It's just a matter of spending a few weeks learning the process, using this book and also the online audio guidance if you want more help in the learning process – and then applying the technique where needed.

THE FIRST METHOD:
WAKING UP AT WORK

Here's the complete Wake Up training program that you will want to move through over and over as you master this dimension of our Take Charge program. Remember when you want extra guidance to go online at http://takecharge-training.com and be guided effortlessly through this same verbal script. Power comes through practice!

At first, the process will take three to four minutes – but once you establish this new habit of mind, you can move through the process in less than a minute. Because this Wake Up process is also the beginning of the Take Charge method, we'll be returning often to make sure that you truly are mastering the experience, as follows:

Just relax and make yourself comfortable . . . stretch a bit if you want . . . yawn perhaps . . . and choose to turn your mind's attention toward your whole-body Wake Up experience, here in this present moment . . .

Say to yourself, "I feel the air flowing in and out of my nose," and allow those words to tune your attention into that sensory experience . . . the air flowing in . . . the air flowing out . . . expand your awareness to include the volume inside your head . . . relax your jaw . . . your tongue . . . your facial muscles . . . let your thoughts become quiet . . . and begin to allow a feeling of peacefulness to fill your mind . . .

And as you stay fully aware of the sensation of the air flowing in and out your nose, say to yourself: "I also feel the movements in my chest and belly," and expand your awareness to include those movements. Make no effort to breathe . . . experience the feeling of volume inside your chest and belly, expanding and contracting with each breath . . .

And now to wake up empathy, say to yourself, "I'm also aware of the feelings in my heart," and experience whatever feelings you find in your heart, right in the middle of your breathing . . . accept your present feelings . . . breathe into them . . . shine your attention upon them . . . let them . . . relax . . . change . . . expand . . . and to encourage good feelings in your heart, remember a friend, family member, or lover for whom you feel love . . . let that good feeling fill your heart . . .

And now say, "I'm aware of my whole body at once, here in this present moment," and allow your awareness to include your feet . . . your hands . . . your knees . . . your head . . . your back . . . your toes . . . your heart . . . your breathing . . . your skin . . . your whole body, here in this present moment . . .

Your breathing is now full and relaxed . . . your mind

quiet . . . your heart feels good . . . your whole body feels "in the zone" . . . and you can open up to any insights that might come to you . . . any creative flashes . . . set your mind free . . . be open to a new experience . . .

Now, you can begin perhaps to stretch a bit, open your eyes if they're closed . . . and as you move back into full engagement with your workplace, you can bring with you any insights that might have come . . . you can continue to feel relaxed . . . strong . . . friendly . . . alert . . . creative . . . and in harmony with your team . . .

PAUSE & EXPERIENCE

Review

One: I feel the air flowing in and out of my nose.

Two: I feel the movements in my chest and belly as I breathe.

Three: I'm aware of the feelings in my heart.

Four: I'm aware of my whole body, here in this present moment.

PART TWO

Shifting into Peak Performance

Nothing at last is sacred
but the integrity
of your own mind.
- Ralph Waldo Emerson

CHAPTER 2

FEEL GREAT AT WORK

FEEL GOOD

CHAPTER 2: PREVIEW

Core Need – Feeling Good: Do you want to feel happier at work but find it difficult to achieve? You are probably one of the countless numbers of people who are victims of profound mood swings over which they seem to have little control. Perhaps your greatest need is learning how to control your moods and feel good whenever and wherever you want. Imagine being able to move to an upbeat mood, increase your energy, feel more positive, and improve your performance.

Our Solution: Your moods are dependent on the thoughts and images you let run through your mind. To take charge of your mood swings, you need to quiet negative thought-flows and refocus your attention in directions that stimulate good feelings throughout your body. This chapter advances the Wake Up process by teaching this "feel great" refocusing skill.

The Process: At any given moment, you can feel good. In this chapter, you will learn the skill of redirecting your attention so that you discover the good feelings you already have and let go of bad ones.

Your Payoff: The payoff is great – because when you feel bad you drag down your entire team as well as yourself. When you shift into feeling good, you raise team spirit and boost your performance and sense of well-being.

FEEL GOOD

DILEMMA AT WORK

Karen is a healthcare sales executive in her late thirties. She has diligently mastered all the technical and business skills needed to make her a top salesperson – but somehow she still lacks the passion and easy rapport that successful salespeople possess. Her problem is that she never lets herself actually enjoy her work. She's so worried about success, and tense with applying all her great sales techniques, that her habitual mood is negative rather than positive. Feeling unhappy inside, she's not able to be genuinely friendly – and her customers therefore feel uncomfortable in her presence.

Karen's direct solution to her work problem is to realize that she can act from the inside to shift from low, tense moods into an enjoyable experience of the present moment. When she takes just a few minutes a day to master the Wake Up process, and also the first step of the Take Charge methods, she'll be able to choose to feel good as she goes about her selling. And she'll not only succeed, but also fully enjoy the process.

In earlier times, traditional corporate strategies for accelerating productivity almost never encouraged employees to relax and feel good. You came to the office to work and delayed feelings of calm and pleasure to the weekend. Work was supposed to be nonstop labor, with employees tensely struggling for higher productivity and greater achievement. Employees and executives alike were encouraged to push and strain and worry their way toward success, not relax and enjoy the process. Work has traditionally been seen as a means to an end, a necessary evil to earn a living. Yet what if work were also an end itself, an activity that was both enjoyable and fulfilling – an essential setting for our own personal development? What if we could shatter the old divide between work and "real life" and integrate them into one inspiring whole?

Our method shows you the way forward and is supported by evidence from psychological research indicating that we perform best when we feel good in our bodies – not when we hold ourselves chronically locked in tense thoughts and dull dissatisfied emotions.

When we feel physically and emotionally good, our breathing naturally deepens, we get more oxygen to the brain, and our mental performance improves. When we relax and shift into a more expansive mind state, our higher integrative mental functions are activated – and we come up with insights that make our day. In general, when we enjoy our work, we naturally tend to be more productive, to relate better, and flash with new insights.

What does it actually take to feel good – as opposed to feeling down or bad, or feeling numb and nothing at all? First, good feelings are experienced as sensations in your body, not as thoughts in your mind. Feeling good therefore requires being aware of your body in the present moment – feeling good is always a here-and-now event, a sensory happening.

FEEL GOOD

So always, the first step toward feeling better is to choose to turn your mind's attention toward the general source of good feelings in your body right now. How can you best accomplish this shifting of your focus in directions that make you feel better? What is the mental tool that will enable you to succeed in this shift toward good feelings?

The answer is the Focus Phrase – a short, concise verbal sentence that clearly states your intent to redirect your attention in a particular direction and that, when you actually say the statement, stimulates this shift.

FOCUS-PHRASE TECHNOLOGY

Cognitive research has shown that your mind will quite willingly respond and do what you tell it to do – but you must first state your intent and employ a carefully selected phrase or set of phrases that will predictably provoke the desired inner response.

We are always using focus phrases, whether we know it or not. They are like habitual scripts or "self-talk." Typically, they are unconscious and negative. They include phrases such as "I am never going to be successful in this job"; "I am in the wrong career"; "Nobody likes me in the office"; "Nobody takes notice of me"; or "I am not a creative person."

You inherited most of these phrases from your childhood, from your parents and school. Our method is designed to make you aware of these damaging focus phrases, to help you stop saying them to yourself and then choose to replace them with positive ones.

You now have the choice to write a new script and use phrases which will move you forward toward higher levels of performance and happiness. This is how you make genuine, long-term changes in your life.

For instance, when you choose to shift from being lost in distracting thoughts and emotions to enjoying a breath of fresh air in the present moment, you immediately change your awareness. Studies show that the best "point of entry" for this change is your breathing (as you've already begun to explore for yourself). And the most direct and powerful words to effect an instant shift into awareness of your breathing are: "I feel the air flowing in and out of my nose."

This basic statement of intent seems short and simple, and that's exactly what we want. In order to make a major change in your inner experience at work, often right in the middle of a tense situation, you're going to need a Focus Phrase that is as short and simple as possible. State exactly what you want to do – and do it.

Focus Phrases are not designed to initiate deep thought or subtle reflection – they're designed to stimulate immediately a particular shift in your focus of attention. All you have to do is remember to say the words, and let them provoke the desired shift.

As a general rule, you won't want to say these Focus Phrases out loud so that others can hear you. Instead, you'll say these statements of intent "to yourself" – which means that you'll feel

FEEL GOOD

subtle sensations of speech in your vocal cords and throat, but you won't actually vocalize the words out loud.

This is a very important point, because if you just "think the words," almost nothing will happen. There's a particular power that comes into being through the act of actually saying words, rather than just thinking them. Thinking happens only in your mind. Speaking (even inaudibly) is a whole-body happening in the present moment. Your power of intent is greatly increased when you move from thinking to speaking your intent.

> You'll be amazed, as you become effective at this method, that your mind learns to shift dramatically in the direction the Focus Phrase aims your attention. That's the unique dynamic of Focus Phrase technology.

THE PROCESS IN ACTION

In this chapter, we're exploring how you can quickly shift in the direction of feeling better at work. You're going to learn a new Focus Phrase that directly encourages good feelings at work. And we're going to explore how the four Focus Phrases of the Wake Up method also directly help you shift into a more enjoyable, empowered, friendly state of mind. For instance, saying "I feel the air flowing in and out of my nose" stimulates a major revolution in how you feel – a cognitive shift away from inner thoughts, toward present-moment experience.

Imagine you're working at your desk or waiting for an appointment, maybe on hold on the phone or serving customers, or in a meeting – and you realize that you've dropped low, mentally and emotionally. Furthermore, you're not feeling at all good inside your own skin.

Choosing to shift into a more creative, enjoyable, charismatic presence, you say to yourself, "I feel the air flowing in and out of my nose," and not only do you tune in to the physiological sensations of the air flowing in and out – you also experience a general expansion of consciousness so that you pop into the ever-changing reality of the present moment. You regain your senses.

Your emotions are expressed directly in your breathing – which at any moment is either tense or relaxed, uptight or expansive, inspired or depressed. That's why, if you want to take charge of how you feel, you must first turn your focus to your breathing. Try it again for yourself – even as you read these words, say to yourself, "I feel the air flowing in and out of my nose," and notice that, by saying the words, your attention does effortlessly shift to that sensory experience.

Gaining a Dimension

Here's a most curious realization – there is, in fact, no volume, no depth, no perspective, nor sensation at all, in pure thought. Thoughts are symbols and, as such, they don't exist anywhere but in the linear thought-flows of your own cogitative mind.

The experience of your senses, however, is three-dimensional – because it tunes you in to "out there" in the real world of space

FEEL GOOD

and time. When you shift into thinking mode inside your brain, you actually drop down in a spatial contraction from three-dimensional sensory reality into two-dimensional symbolic reality.

Yes, problem-solving and brainstorming are great tools for making plans, generating strategy, and reflecting on the direction of your company or the meaning of life. But there's just nothing quite like suddenly shifting out of the two-dimensional world of your thoughts and popping back into the actual three-dimensional experience of being vitally alive in your body.

Especially after some initial training, you'll find that as soon as you tune in to your breath experience in your nose, you also become conscious of your jaw and tongue, and the facial muscles around your eyes – and if there's any tension in these muscles, they'll thankfully start to relax. The contraction and tension ease up, you find yourself feeling better – and all it took was one conscious breath plus one potent Focus Phrase.

QUIETING YOUR THOUGHTS

Your own thoughts often make you feel bad. Worries, problems, time pressures, angry and frustrated thoughts – you, like everyone else, torment yourself with the seemingly nonstop chatter in your mind. To feel better, you can advance with the second Focus Phrase and, with your awareness, follow the air down into your lungs and experience the actual sensations of the movements being generated in the chest and belly, with each breath.

Studies at the National Institutes of Health have shown that you cannot continue with a logical stream of thought and at the same time focus your attention on two or more sensory experiences – and that's exactly what you do when you expand your awareness to include the movements in your chest and belly as you breathe. You quiet your mind . . .

Have you ever wondered why listening to stereo recordings of music transports you outside your usual thoughts and feelings, and shifts you into a most wonderful transcendent state? Consider the complex intertwined melodies and harmonies of Bach or the Beatles – when you fully focus on two or more harmonies in music, psychologically, you are, in effect, short-circuiting your chronic thought-flows and entering a state of mind where your thoughts are quiet and your mood uplifted.

Except for on these special occasions, quieting that nonstop stream of thoughts and images in your mind has always been easier said than done. Traditional meditative "quiet mind" techniques often take ten years rather than two weeks to master. The good news is that perceptual psychology has discovered a way for anyone anywhere to quiet all thoughts immediately – by focusing one's attention on two different sensory inputs at the same time.

First, you say, "I feel the air flowing in and out of my nose," and experience that sensation for a breath or two. Then you say, "I also feel the movements in my chest and belly as I breathe,"

FEEL GOOD

and allow your awareness to expand to include all the sensations in your chest and belly, generated by your inhalations and exhalations.

Suddenly, you're focusing on two (actually a great many) sensations in your body at once. Predictably, your flow of thoughts ceases temporarily as your awareness expands to include your head, your chest, and your belly – all at once.

> This mental pop from thought to experience can be dramatic because it instantly brings you into a direct encounter with the present moment.

Mastering this two-step mental shift, like mastering anything, takes a bit of practice. We're here to guide you through the basic inner process over and over, especially online, to make sure that in the next couple of weeks you really "get" this process and make it your own. Practice does make perfect, and that's what we're aiming toward – full mastery of this new mind-management technique.

HEART POWER

Can you imagine the difference between relating to someone who is out of touch with the feelings in their heart, who's numb or cold or just not there emotionally – versus relating to someone who is tuned in to positive heartfelt feelings of acceptance, empathy, and team spirit? Who makes you feel better?

If you're not careful, that cold, heartless person just might be you. When you don't actively remember to tune in to your heart and nurture good feelings inside you, then there is the possibility that you will be distant and fail to engage effectively with those around you. Furthermore, you simply won't feel good at all.

You might not associate your work with feelings in your heart. Such feelings probably feel more appropriate for life at home with your family.

Yet imagine how great work could be if you could genuinely act from the heart and build authentic friendships with your colleagues and customers. Imagine if you could achieve those same profound emotions of compassion, happiness, and peace at work that you feel with your loved ones.

Then imagine how much more effective you would be in your work if you felt truly supported and cared for by your colleagues. How much better would that be than the fear, anxiety, and competition that characterizes most organizations?

Well, it all starts with you. Once you start to listen to and act from your heart, people start to respond positively to you. You start to see and treat others as real people, not just "objects" that are there to be manipulated for you to achieve your goals. This adds a wonderful dimension to every activity, and greatly enriches your work experience.

The third expansion, "I'm aware of the feelings in my heart," greatly increases your emotional warmth and empathy. The difference between being unaware and out of touch with your feelings and being purposefully tuned into your empathic powers is like night and day.

FEEL GOOD

Most of us agree that living life devoid of any warm, compassionate feelings in the heart would be no life at all. Our hearts are where we experience the feelings of love, trust, wisdom, hope, joy, and belonging. Why deny ourselves these incredible feelings for the 48 weeks or so we are at work each year? In fact, especially in sales and service positions, staying attuned to positive feelings in our hearts is what makes us bond with customers and flourish in sales.

The good news is that we can experience these feelings at work today, and forevermore. This is the essence of "emotional intelligence," which is vital to long-term success and fulfillment at work. In this chapter and others to come, we're aiming to help you develop your emotional intelligence – so you can have more self-awareness, empathy, and rapport with others. This will generate team spirit, creative insight, cooperation, and that deep sense of knowing that your business decisions are harmonious and trustworthy.

So – what can you do right now and every day to shift from feeling numb or cold or hard or disconnected from your feelings to directly plugging in to the power of your empathy and emotional warmth on the job? How can you choose to feel good at work?

Simply memorize the special Focus Phrase that expands your mind's awareness to include what you want to focus on. Say to yourself, "I'm aware of the feelings in my heart," and let those words work their associative magic and expand your awareness so that, right in the middle of your breath experience, you encounter whatever feelings might be in your heart at that moment.

Please note that these Focus Phrases are not being used as positive affirmations. In this program, we never use positive affirmations because they tend to fly in the face of reality – and that's almost always counterproductive if not downright foolish.

> Focus Phrases are essential reminders
> to use your inner power and take charge
> of your thinking, emotions, and moods.

Focus Phrases as used in this method remind you of realistic valuable directions to aim your power of attention. They are your own reminder system, which regularly returns your attention to the experiences and mental functions that serve you best. Each one is designed to focus your attention on a vital cognitive activity for your success and well-being at work. Each one accesses a specific inner resource, and cumulatively they move you into your optimum state of performance.

Right now, if you say, "I'm aware of the feelings in my heart," you're choosing to direct your mind's awareness directly toward whatever feelings are present in your heart. Sometimes you'll turn your attention to your heart and find painful, depressing, anxious, or angry feelings that are spoiling your mental clarity,

FEEL GOOD

communication, and creative abilities. You might therefore want to look away and avoid these feelings – but here's a crucial psychological fact: Whether you notice them or not, these feelings will drag you down at work. And simply ignoring them doesn't make them go away. It only allows them to fester and disrupt everything you do.

Here's the good news. As soon as you say to yourself, "I'm aware of the feelings in my heart," and consciously turn your mind's loving attention inward, something almost magical begins to happen. Your old negative emotions will, step by step, over a few weeks, begin to lose their hold on you, as your heart starts to recover and to heal. You act in the direction of feeling better.

FEEL GOOD – NOW

Curiously, you don't need to move slowly through this process for it to be effective – in fact, our program is designed to be done quite quickly. You don't linger for long on any of the mental shifts; you just jump in and do them, and then move on.

Why the speed? Two reasons: first, so that you can use this method right in middle of a frantic workday; and second – and this has been quite a surprise for psychologists – this process actually works best when you move through it rapidly without dwelling too long on any one step.

The Focus Phrase process is cumulative: Each new one builds on previous ones, so that each step takes you deeper into the full power and impact of the process. And we've found that it's better to take just a minute or two often each day to move through the process, rather than taking half an hour and doing it just once a day.

Once you've turned your attention toward the source of good feelings in your breathing and heart, the next logical step is to feel good in your whole body all at once. The fourth step of the Wake Up process expands your awareness a final physical notch and brings you fully "into the zone" as a conscious integrated presence – enabling you to make fast contact with your higher levels of awareness and wisdom, while also waking up to whole-body pleasure in the present moment.

Being "in the zone" means expanding into an experience of wholeness and integration where you're aware of your entire being at once. The total you!

What words activate this expansion? Definitely, the fourth Wake Up Focus Phrase: "I'm aware of my whole body at once, here in this present moment." As you say the words and your awareness expands to include your whole self, you effortlessly attain an integrated physical and emotional presence that makes strong contact with the people around you and also grounds you in your own core integrity and power.

This expanded state of pleasurable awareness is exactly opposite to the mental state of Karen in our business example. She habitually lived in a contracted state in her head, where she wasn't conscious of her physical presence at all. And when she did tune into her body, she found it anxious and tense and not feeling good at all.

In this negative state, she didn't enjoy the process of listening, of relating to her customers and developing rapport. And with her worried thoughts and manipulative sales plans, her inner stress was chronically high, sapping her energy and draining her empathy and capacity for enjoyment.

What a difference Karen found in her work when she began regularly talking to herself just before a sales meeting, using the four Wake Up Focus Phrases plus the first Take Charge Focus Phrase to turn her mind's attention immediately to her experience in the present moment. As she learned to focus outward and acknowledge the presence of people she was dealing with, she found she could perceive their feelings and needs and develop solutions for them, rather than just going through the routine of selling products. And when she felt good in her body, she discovered that sales soared.

You'll discover that you can also benefit greatly when at work you regularly give yourself breaks from your mind, shift into whole-body awareness – and tap all the dimensions of your power and well-being that are inactive when you're caught up inside your mind. Here's the basic process you're presently learning:

Give yourself permission to stretch a bit . . . yawn perhaps . . . and tune in to the air flowing in and out of your nose . . . be aware of the space and volume inside your head . . . allow your jaw to relax, your tongue . . . and as you stay aware of the sensation of the air flowing in and out of your nose, expand your awareness to include the movements in your chest and belly as you breathe . . . experience the volume inside your chest and belly, expanding and contracting with each breath . . .

And now, also be aware of the feelings in your heart, right in the middle of your breathing . . . accept your feelings . . . breathe into them . . . shine your loving attention on them . . . and to encourage good feelings in your heart, remember someone you feel love for . . . let that love expand in your heart . . .

And now say, "I'm aware of my whole body at once, here in this present moment," and allow your awareness to expand to include your feet . . . your hands . . . your knees . . . your head . . . your back . . . your toes . . . your heart . . . your breathing . . . your skin . . . your whole body . . . here in this present moment . . .

PAUSE & EXPERIENCE

FEEL GOOD

PERMISSION TO FEEL GOOD

When you have a full minute to move through that Wake Up process, great. But sometimes you'll find that you need something even faster. Karen learned that when she was waiting to see a customer and felt nervous while imagining all sorts of conflicts that might develop, she could indeed take charge of her mind and in just one minute expand into the Wake Up "in the zone" quality of consciousness.

But sometimes, right in the middle of a sales meeting, she'd suddenly lose her expanded confident stance and contract back into her habitual tensions. What could she do, almost instantly, to regain her composure and charisma?

We now come to the first step of the Take Charge method, which compresses the four steps of the Wake Up process into a super-fast cognitive-shifting experience. When you have time, of course it's always best to move through the four Focus Phrases of the Wake Up method, as just reviewed. But when you're right in the heat of battle at work, you can also do the following:

1. TURN YOUR MIND'S ATTENTION TO YOUR NEXT EXHALE . . . AND CONTINUE EXHALING UNTIL YOU'RE EMPTY OF AIR . . .

2. WHILE EMPTY OF AIR, SAY TO YOURSELF, "I GIVE MYSELF PERMISSION TO FEEL GOOD!" LET THESE WORDS POINT YOUR MIND'S ATTENTION TOWARD

GOOD SENSATIONS IN YOUR BODY, AS YOU REALLY GET HUNGRY FOR YOUR NEXT INHALE . . .

3. SURRENDER TO YOUR DEEP URGE TO INHALE, AND LET THE AIR COME FLOWING FAST IN THROUGH YOUR NOSE (FEEL THIS!), AND ON DOWN DEEP INTO YOUR CHEST AND BELLY (FEEL THIS!). KEEP EXPANDING TO INCLUDE THE FEELINGS IN YOUR HEART — AND YOUR WHOLE BODY, HERE IN THIS PRESENT MOMENT. ALL IN JUST ONE BREATH!

After a few weeks of training, when Karen did this "Permission to feel good!" single-breath act, she found she could shift her mind's attention in just one breath away from mental tensions and emotional stress, toward her inner center of power and pleasure. She directly overrode her anxious tense thoughts with the liberating statement, "I give myself permission to feel good."

> When you say to yourself, "I give myself permission to feel good," you immediately start to feel relaxed and alert – which is your natural state.

The act of giving yourself permission to feel good is perhaps the most important act you can regularly make at work – because when you feel good, you're naturally in optimum mental and emotional condition to deal with anything at work, or at home.

At any given moment, there are literally hundreds of directions in which you can aim your power of attention that will make you feel bad. There are so many things you can worry about, or get angry about, or feel depressed about in your present life or in the past or the future. And you have the choice, each new moment, of breaking free from habits that fixate your attention on things that make you feel bad. Instead, you can state your positive intent and then focus your attention toward that basic experience of feeling good inside your own skin.

Each time you exhale, say to yourself, "I give myself permission to feel good," and then inhale with your mind quiet and alert to new experience, you'll find that the words have more and more immediate power to point your mind's attention toward all the good feelings that are happening right now in your body – but to which you're not paying any attention.

Feeling good is a state of being – emotions, heart, body, and soul. You don't have to be doing something to feel good – just be aware of the moment.

Feeling good is an inner quality that comes when your mind is quiet and you're tuned in to your physical presence. It's a quality of consciousness in which you let go of the future, let go of anxious imaginings, let go of guilt and shame and all the other self-inflicted negative emotions.

Feeling good emerges naturally when you're relaxed, focused here in the present moment, enjoying your own presence, free to move a bit if you want to, free to breathe deeply – feeling good is your natural state when you're not tormenting yourself with negative thoughts.

And notice – there's almost never anyone stopping you from doing this. It's your own mind that holds you prisoner and denies you pleasure at work. But even though good feelings are always just a breath away, even though you have a vast potential for experiencing pleasure in your body and emotions, no one else can give you permission to feel good. You must do this for yourself.

SAY IT – DO IT!

Each day – often – remember to pause and say to yourself, "I give myself permission to feel good," or perhaps, "I choose to wake up and feel good," if these words work better for you. The level or intensity of the good feeling is not what's important here – what's important is turning your mind's attention away from all the things that habitually pull you down and looking instead in a more positive, uplifting direction.

Say it – do it. It's so simple!

Don't spend any more time ruminating or worrying, don't waste your life failing to go into action. And don't try to imagine what it will be like. At some point, you need just to jump in and begin moving through this cognitive-shifting process designed to set you free to feel good in the here and now.

FEEL GOOD

TAKE CHARGE UPLIFT 1:
FEELING GOOD!

Let's formally move through the full "Wake Up/Feel Good" process that you'll be learning by heart over the next weeks.

First of all, let's walk again through the four-step Wake Up experience, which is always the preparation for beginning the Take Charge method. Hold in mind that you will never have the same experience twice – so be open as always to a new encounter with the ever-surprising present moment.

"I feel the air flowing in and out of my nose"

. . . experience this deeply on the inhale.

"I feel the movements in my chest and belly"

. . . experience this deeply on the inhale.

"I'm aware of the feelings in my heart"

. . . experience this deeply on the inhale.

"I'm aware of my whole body at once"

. . . experience this deeply on the inhale.

TAKE CHARGE 1:
PERMISSION TO FEEL GOOD!

Now let's do basically the same awareness-shifting, using the first step in the Take Charge method in which you build on your training with the Wake Up process and almost instantaneously expand into whole-body awareness and pleasure:

Exhale . . . and hold your breath on empty.

Say to yourself, "I give myself permission to feel good."

Allow your next inhalation to come rushing in on its own.

Tune in to the movements in your chest and belly.

Experience the feelings in your heart.

Be aware of your whole body in this present moment.

Say again, "I give myself permission to feel good!"

PAUSE & EXPERIENCE

C H A P T E R 3

ACT WITH CONFIDENCE

STOP WORRYING

CHAPTER 3: PREVIEW

Core Need – Act with Confidence: The modern workplace can be seriously anxiety-provoking. For the sake of your career and health, it's essential to learn how to handle uncertainties and stress, and master special skills that enable you to stay confident and calm even during the most challenging situations and crises. Effective anxiety management is a foundation of success.

Our Solution: We offer specific skills that enable you to recognize when your thoughts are causing worried and uncertain emotions – and empower you to redirect your attention to your inner clarity and confidence. You become the master of situations that otherwise might upset or overwhelm you.

The Process: Our Take Charge method includes the step of consciously "saying no" to your worries, shifting out of thoughts that don't serve you, and choosing to focus your power of attention in directions that bring a feeling of peace right in the middle of a hectic workday.

Your Payoff: Once you learn to manage your moods effectively and remain mostly anxiety-free at work, you tap new reserves of energy and achieve more. You'll also be highly regarded by your colleagues for your balance and composure, and improve your capacity for leadership.

STOP WORRYING

DILEMMA AT WORK

Richard rose fast as a manager for a Fortune 500 technology corporation – but now has hit a plateau he can't progress beyond. His problem is that, although he's creative and communicates effectively, he habitually undermines his own confidence by worrying about possible negative scenarios – rather than trusting himself and pushing for success. His anxiety habits not only inhibit his performance, but also people around him don't like his chronic worrying and some even prefer not to work with him.

Richard is like so many executives and employees. He is stuck in a comfort zone of his own making, limited by fears of failure, rejection, and even success. He has imprisoned himself with anxieties which rise to the surface at critical moments. In these moments, which will determine his career, he must learn to master the skill of silencing these habitual anxious thoughts – by practicing the second step of the Take Charge method diligently. In this way, whenever worries start to undermine his confidence, he can quietly act inside his mind to shift from anxious to confident. As he gains more peace of mind, he'll also be able to tap higher levels of creativity and strategic thinking.

We all know that nothing saps our energy, creativity, and overall productivity at work as often and seriously as chronic anxiety. Yet most people spend a great deal of their day worrying – about their job, health, finances, and family.

How about you – do you often find yourself caught up in

worried thoughts and projections? Do you worry mostly about important issues, or also not-so-important issues? And does worrying knock down your sense of confidence, strength, and well-being?

As you know, when you are caught up in worried thoughts and imaginings, your whole body gets hit with the resulting stress and weakness of the basic fear response. If this is prolonged, you end up feeling shaky, uncertain, weak, confused, unfocused, and downright upset and anxious – and this undermines your physical well-being. It's vital to realize the impact of worrying on your work performance and mood at work, and act to do something every day to minimize your habitual fixations on anxious thoughts and imaginings.

An unspoken agreement at work is that you leave your personal worries at the door when you arrive at work. This might sound cruel, but it's simply a necessity for getting work done. Furthermore, as mentioned earlier, worrying about work-related issues is also usually counterproductive.

Worrying achieves little or nothing and over a period of time will severely undermine your performance at work. For instance, if you are a sales executive, no one will employ you if you overtly worry about personal or even business concerns. Worry makes buyers uneasy and uncertain, which jeopardizes the sale. The same is true in other areas. If you work in service, anxiety puts customers on edge. If you are a manager, it undermines your credibility and charisma.

The Take Charge Process trains you how to use your inner power to shift from anxiety to peace of mind.

First of all, the Wake Up step in our program helps lift your state of mind away from worrying as you shift into present-moment sensory awareness. You'll find that sometimes just moving through this short process is all you need – you become fully present and your mind is at peace, your heart feels expansive, and you're in touch with your deeper intuitive creative powers. Fine – just carry on with whatever you're doing, in this expanded state.

Most people, however, find that all too often, after they move through the Wake Up expansion into whole-body awareness, in just a few moments they tend to slip back into a less conscious state as they sink again into old worry habits. To deal with this dilemma, we offer the full Take Charge process, to ensure a lasting change of heart and mind.

So even while you're practicing the Wake Up process, you can move on to the second Take Charge expansion and shift your mind into a more peaceful state, which will improve your mood and boost your energy level.

STOP WORRYING

You feel anxious when you worry about something bad that might happen to you. Psychologically, anxiety is a fear-based fantasy projection into the future. You can short-circuit your worry habits by shifting your mind's attention to the present and then using a potent Focus Phrase, clearly declaring to yourself your intent to let go of your worries. Again – say it, do it.

FEELINGS IN YOUR HEAD

If you're caught in fear-based thoughts that grip you and make you anxious about something that might happen in the future, or if you have what Sigmund Freud called "free-floating anxiety," where you're just generally afraid something bad might happen any moment, you'll find that the muscles of your scalp will be tense and often downright painful. This occurs in the area surrounding your brain, rather than inside it.

This general area in your head experiences an entire array of feelings. Sometimes your head feels good, expansive, light, and at peace, caught up in a general bodily sensation of well-being and even bliss. But at other times, your head can ache terribly, or your jaw muscles can be painfully tense.

In general, your head responds and reacts physically
to one of two primary emotions: fear or peace.
When you're afraid, caught in worries, and stuck
in anxiety, tension grips the muscles of your skull
and neck. Conversely, when you feel that everything's
okay, your scalp muscles relax and you feel a warm
sensation of peace and pleasure in your head.

STOP WORRYING

Those recurrent muscular aches and tensions of your head are
habitual. Far too many people go through their average workday
with their scalp tense and neck muscles cramped. The muscular
tensions are maintained by mostly unconscious negative one-
liners that provoke chronic worrying. "Something bad is liable to
happen to me at any minute" sums up these one-liners that
plague our minds.

If we don't act to override our chronic worries and tensions,
then we're just stuck with them – and that's totally nonproductive
and no fun at all. Therefore, it's time to do something to break
free from this at-work tension. Here's an initial experience in the
right direction:

Tune in to your breathing . . . feel the air flowing in and out of your nose . . . and also notice how your head feels right now . . . breathe into whatever feelings you find in your head . . . notice if you're holding jaw muscles tight . . . scalp muscles tense . . . eye muscles and tongue contracted.

Now say to yourself, "I give myself permission to feel good," and as you exhale, sigh . . . relax your tongue and jaws . . . move your head gently from side to side . . . and allow the muscular tensions you find throughout your head to relax a bit . . . give your head permission to feel better . . .

PAUSE & EXPERIENCE

SAY IT . . . SAY IT . . . SAY IT

As noted, your thinking mind seems to run nonstop throughout each new day. Thoughts and images continue to flow through the mind – and all too often those thoughts are negative, focused on ideas and memories that, in turn, stimulate negative emotions, which, in turn, provoke upset tensions in your physical body.

As mentioned earlier, it's vital to realize that most of your ongoing inner suffering isn't being caused directly by the outside world. Most of your emotional suffering is being caused by those thoughts that run through your head. When you realize this, you take one of the great leaps toward improving the quality of your life.

The voice that you hear constantly talking inside your head is often called the ego. Out of habit or provocation, the ego will think of something that you should do, and state this need with words such as "I need to get up and check my email." Or perhaps, responding to an upset, angry colleague, it might think, "I'm in danger and need to protect myself."

If you watch your mind in action, you'll discover that, except for when you operate on automatic pilot, most of your actions and, indeed, most of your emotions are being directly stimulated by thoughts that run through your mind. This is just how we work – we are usually ego-driven.

Most meditation programs from ancient traditions see the ego as the bad guy you must silence before you can find peace of mind. We studied these meditative mind-management techniques for a number of years – but finally realized that for most people, it's pointless to do battle against the ego and its constant chatter.

Rather, the best approach seems to be to use mental judo. Use the power of the ego to go with the thought-flow, and gently redirect that flow of thoughts in directions that serve you. The Focus Phrases you're learning do just that.

STOP WORRYING

Instead of trying to make the ego stop thinking entirely and somehow silence all the worried thoughts that make you tense and anxious, the Take Charge program prefers to give the ego something really important to do – namely, to memorize and remember to say the various Focus Phrases (there are 11 in all) on a regular basis and thus shift your attention away from fear-based thoughts, toward success-based thoughts.

After all, when it comes right down to it, who is going to decide to say the Focus Phrases? That's right – your ego, that thinking, judging "director" of your mind. And we're finding that honoring the ego, through conscious positive employment of the thinking/talking part of the mind, works emotional and mental wonders. Rather than doing battle to silence negative thoughts, you can instead encourage vocalization of very specific positive thoughts that redirect attention in successful directions.

Your ego voice carries great power.
When your ego voice speaks,
the rest of you tends to listen
and to do what it's told, right?
So let's use this natural power,
in a conscious way that
will transform your life.

Time again for action – say it, do it! State exactly what you want to have happen, in terms of anxiety reduction and engendering feelings of peace and calm in your mind. Just go ahead and do it . . . say to yourself on your next exhalation, "I let go of all my worries . . . and feel peaceful in my mind."

PAUSE & EXPERIENCE

PEACE AT WORK

People are mostly conditioned to think that work must be hectic and a constant struggle in order for success to happen. In this book, we would like to counter that old assumption – because, psychologically, it's simply not valid. Yes, there are times when we must get up a head of steam and plunge into a difficult situation, take on the stress and move through it. But there are so many other times on the job when a peaceful, clear mind and positive calm emotions can do a much better job than tense, anxious, confused states of mind.

You know that point when you're brooding over a problem even though your mind feels burnt, your emotions tense, your breathing tight – you push further and further in that direction because you believe you have to maintain the tension and the stress in order to make your breakthrough. You certainly don't want to be caught sitting calmly at your desk while everybody else is in an uproar over a difficulty at work, do you?

STOP WORRYING

Well, actually, you do. Because through your calmness, you'll be the one who shifts into a more expansive state of mind and emotion, from which insights and breakthroughs tend to emerge. Over and over, flashes of inspiration come into being right at that moment when you finally give up, surrender, and relax . . . then pow! All at once you see the whole of the picture, a creative vision flashes in your mind – and you've got it!

> Your ego is smart; it's not at all dumb. Therefore, in our Take Charge approach to high performance, the aim is not to try to fight the ego when it gets caught in worries and conflicts – but to remind it that there is another way to go about success at work.

In this book, you're learning to use your ego and not let it use you. As you practice the Take Charge process, your ego is learning each step of the way that there are, indeed, alternate ways to be effective. Your ego naturally wants to help and protect you. The problem is that it is using inappropriate methods for doing this, such as fight-or-flight strategies based on fear. Now you are teaching it better choices and methods.

We assure you that, after just a week or so of practicing the Focus Phrases and experiencing their positive effect, the inner voice that guides your attention and your actions is going to begin to change its tune. More and more often, it's going to remember to say the magic words, "I let go of my worries and feel peaceful in my mind." Why will your ego begin to sing a new tune? Because it will observe that as you say these words and respond to them, good things happen.

As you say, "I let go of my worries," and shift more fully into the present moment, you act directly to free yourself from the anxious thoughts gripping your mind and body. And when you become competent at this and say, "I feel peaceful in my mind," you'll feel that peace instantly.

Saying is doing. So over and over, practice this on your own.

After reading this paragraph, see if you have memorized the two Focus Phrases "I give myself permission to feel good" and "I let go of my worries and feel peaceful in my mind." I encourage you to put the book aside just for six to ten breaths, close your eyes if you want to, and say the two Focus Phrases one after the other, on exhalations . . . several times . . . and allow the power of your ego's spoken intent to begin to take hold within you and generate the desired changes in the feelings in your head and your whole body:

"I give myself permission to feel good."

"I let go of my worries and feel peaceful in my mind."

PAUSE & EXPERIENCE

STOP WORRYING

SUB-VOCAL POWER

These two Focus Phrases are such short simple statements, and yet they carry the associative power, once you have made them your own, to remind you exactly how to focus your mind's attention to elicit an almost instant shift into a better state of mind.

We repeat: These are not positive affirmations. You're not trying to change the world around you magically by wishing it to be different, nor are you trying to change yourself into something different from what you are. You're simply choosing to say words that aim your mind's attention in specific directions you already know, that awaken positive depths and heights of your existing being. You are building new pathways in your mind that will serve you far better than the old ones did.

Notice again how much more powerful it is when you say these words slowly and deliberately to yourself — rather than just thinking about the words alone.

You will always want to "say" rather than just think these Focus Phrases, in order to activate their associative power. Just visualizing them or thinking the words doesn't do it. This method requires a subtle but physical action!

This is particularly valuable at work. For instance, when Richard learned this technique, he was able to use the phrase whenever he needed it, without saying the words out loud. He was certainly too self-conscious to say out loud at a meeting, "I give myself permission to feel good!"

Even though nobody heard Richard as he silently said the words to himself, they saw the results. His breathing deepened and became stronger, his facial muscles relaxed, his eyes became brighter, and his charisma more visible. And when he spoke, his voice carried this inner peace and calm, and gave him that special sense of inner confidence and clarity that great leaders emanate.

Within weeks, Richard looked better and communicated more positively, which increased his confidence dramatically. He was able to stop himself from projecting negative consequences onto everything and started to take risks he'd never taken before. Soon his colleagues, as well as his boss, noticed his new positive attitude, and his career went back on track.

You can achieve the same extraordinary results. Talk to yourself at work. Say the words that turn your attention in directions that empower you, rather than drag you down. See that you have this choice – and act on it – often!

INNER CALM

Peace of mind is almost certainly something you seek and hunger for – because you tend to have so little of it, especially at work. But even though in the past you might seldom have experienced genuine peace of mind as a feeling inside your own head, you know that feeling. So you're not aiming your attention toward something you don't have the potential to achieve. Peace of mind can manifest in your mind at any time – you're just usually focusing your attention elsewhere.

Again, look at this question of choice. At any moment in the hectic frenzy of a busy office, you have the power to turn your mind's attention away from all the thoughts that make you feel tense, worried, and upset, toward a feeling in your mind of peace and calm and "everything's okay right now."

It's your choice. We're giving you the tool that makes that choice always within reach. Just say the one sentence, and your mind will point directly toward where peace is found in your mind. You can immediately experience this truth for yourself. Tune into your breathing, and say, "I let go of all my worries and feel peaceful in my mind," and allow the words to turn your attention away from your worries, toward the peace that dwells within you. Breathe into this peace, hold your focus of attention there, and enjoy the multiple rewards of the shift!

Remember that the Take Charge process is cumulative. Each time you do it, you get better at it. And the first step strengthens the second step as you move into it.

Your consciousness actually does expand when you become

aware of the sensation of the air flowing in and out of your nose and tune into the volume inside your head. It then expands further to include the space in your chest and belly as you breathe and then expands again to include your heart – and then again to include your whole body. And that's just the expansion provoked by the Wake Up process or the Focus Phrase "I give myself permission to feel good"!

Now, while in that expanded state, the next Focus Phrase carries special power to really go deep fast, as you say, "I let go of my worries and feel peaceful in my mind." Notice the careful selection of words here. There is an act first of all – that of letting go. Then there comes a feeling – of peace.

STOP WORRYING

> As you'll discover in the next weeks and months,
> even though your ego loves to talk, it loves
> much more to feel that inner peace that
> comes when its chattering temporarily stops.

There is an extraordinary place of "being" where calm and joy reign just beyond our "thinking." It is a place we knew well as children but then we forgot existed as we spent our lives acquiring knowledge and being rewarded to think, conceptualize, and live in the world of abstractions. And it is only when we balance thinking with being that we can reach our optimal state where success and fulfillment co-exist in harmony.

GETTING THE JOB DONE

When first hearing about encouraging peace of mind on the job, employers and managers sometimes envision their entire workforce sitting around doing nothing. But just the opposite tends to happen – people who are allowed a quick break once an hour to regain their inner peace and composure return to their work at a much higher level of productivity and creativity than when they left it.

Bottom line: It's fun to work when we let go of our worries and tensions, and feel good. There's an inner creative flow that happens naturally when we're allowed to maintain a good feeling in our bodies and peace in our minds.

So we encourage you to take hourly or even half-hourly breaks of one to three minutes, so that you regain your inner integrity and creative power. You'll find online audio programs to guide you in taking these quick Uplifts at work, until you memorize and master these Take Charge pauses and don't need external support. Astute employers will honor your need to put on your earphones at your computer once an hour or even more often, so you can maintain that inner quality of feeling good, at peace, and centered.

Employees who regain their balance respond with improved commitment and performance. A win-win.

The cognitive-shifting process you're learning here not only reduces stress and increases enjoyment on the job – it also allows you to temporarily quiet the flow of thoughts running through your mind.

At first, managers might question how quieting one's mind periodically at work could possibly be a good idea. After all, aren't people paid at work to think? But there are different ways of thinking, and sometimes we need to shift from chronic, deductive thinking to intuitive and creative thinking. The more cognitive strategies we use, the more successful we will be.

We're not saying there isn't a time and place at work for just digging in and getting a boring uncreative job done on time. We all have to do that at work sometimes, regardless of our position. The problem is that we tend to get habitually locked into one type of repetitive thinking and are unable to shift into more creative states and see the whole picture. This greatly reduces our value to our employer and means that we will lag behind our coworkers who know how to regularly take a few breaths, perform a cognitive shift, and expand into whole-body wisdom and leadership.

One of the big competitive advantages for organizations is to harness this potential of their staff to be innovative and creative. And this requires temporary quiet in the mind and full awareness of the body and emotions in the present moment.

Richard discovered this for himself and then turned around and began implementing the Take Charge break throughout his

STOP WORRYING

office – with positive results that boosted his career. Nobody likes to carry worries around all day. When leaders in an organization begin to shed their worries and become more confident and clear-minded, employees tend to follow suit. This is how entire companies can quickly transform their work atmosphere. All it takes to start a Take Charge revolution is one person. And when everyone begins to make the shift, organizations build a culture of excellence grounded in the success, well-being, and fulfillment of each employee.

TAKE CHARGE UPLIFT 2:
CONFIDENCE AND PEACE OF MIND AT WORK

Your job here is to memorize this process and make it your own, so that anywhere, anytime, you can shift into more relaxed, worry-free, creative states of mind. Each time you do this process, you'll establish a deeper habit, so that soon all you need to do is remember the Focus Phrases, say them to yourself in proper order – and allow the associative power of the words to stimulate effortlessly your new experience. Be sure to help yourself to the guidance on our website if you prefer to learn via audio.

STOP WORRYING

Go ahead and get comfortable . . . close your eyes if you want to . . . and say the four Focus Phrases of the Wake Up method: I feel the air flowing in and out of my nose . . . I also feel the movements in my chest and belly as I breathe . . . and I'm aware of the feelings in my heart . . . I'm aware of my whole body, here in this present moment . . .

And now say to yourself, "I give myself permission to feel good."

Exhale until you are empty . . . push with your stomach muscles to get all the air out . . . hold your breath on empty a moment . . . then when you're hungry for air, relax as the new breath comes rushing into your lungs . . .

Stay aware of the feeling of the air flowing in yournose . . . the movements in your chest and belly as you breathe . . .the feelings in your heart . . . be aware of your whole body here in this present moment . . . and also be aware of sounds . . . sights . . . scents . . .

And now for the second expansion of the Take Charge process, say to yourself, "I let go of all my worries and feel peaceful in my mind . . ." Be aware of how you feel in your head . . . relax the tensions in your scalp . . . your tongue and jaw . . . your eyes . . .

Again, say, "I feel peaceful in my mind . . ."

Breathe into whatever peace and quiet you find in your mind right now . . . enjoy the relaxation and inflow of energy . . . be open to new insights . . . and new experience . . .

PAUSE & EXPERIENCE

C H A P T E R 4

COMMUNICATE WITH EMPATHY

EMPATHY BOOST

CHAPTER 4: PREVIEW

Core Need – Communicate with Empathy: Your ability to communicate effectively, build rapport with others, and develop networks and relationships is vital to your career. You need to be an effective communicator to be a valuable asset to your organization. Quality of relationships is perhaps a business's main competitive advantage. In an age where products, services, and prices are so similar, differentiation emerges from the quality of the experience in dealing with the employees of a business.

Our Solution: In this training program, you'll learn to shift into a more empathic mood – through focusing in directions that make you less judgmental, more acceptant, and warm in your relating. You'll learn to boost your emotional intelligence, which will improve your communication performance and well-being.

The Process: Judgmental attitudes can keep your heart closed – and other people experience you as callous and insensitive. Our method will regularly shift your focus of attention to your inner source of empathic emotions, so that you nurture your capacity to relate to others effortlessly.

Your Payoff: When people like you at work, you hold the key to success in whatever you do. Developing nonjudgmental communication will make you more engaging and enable you to make friends and influence people with ease.

DILEMMA AT WORK

Ruth is an administrator in the human resources office of a large bank in Denver. She is highly competent at her job but has been passed over for promotion several times – because she is one of those people who are always casting judgment on everyone around them, colleagues and clients alike. Rather than accepting people, showing empathy, and building solid business relationships, she comes across as cold and distant.

She always seems to look for what is wrong with people and is quick to find fault whenever she can. Her critical attitude makes her colleagues feel uneasy around her and makes them more prone to error, which in turn encourages, and even seems to justify, her criticisms.

For Ruth to address her low empathy and poor relationships at work she will need to learn how to take charge of her own mind, so that she regularly silences the judgmental thoughts that prevent her from getting close to people. Instead, as the Take Charge method teaches, she will actively learn to accept people just as they are – and, in the process, foster mutual friendships that support her personal and career development.

At any given moment of the workday, you can either judge or accept other people. As long as you remain stuck with judgmental thoughts that fuel feelings such as disdain, superiority, hostility, and rejection, you stimulate reactions that involve anger and resentment. When you choose to let go of judgmental thoughts

EMPATHY BOOST

that make people react defensively and aggressively, you tend to evoke feelings of empathy and friendship – again, it's your choice.

But wait, you might say – perhaps you have a legitimate complaint against someone who has just offended and annoyed you. Why shouldn't you hold a grudge against this person; there's a good reason to resent what they've done to you!

Why should you accept people when they've done something wrong or mean? For one very important reason: because holding the emotion of resentment or anger inside you impairs all your communications and interactions, while clouding your mind and disrupting your creative powers.

Maintaining an angry state of judgment does you no good and a lot of harm. Therefore the wise act is always to let go of such judgmental thoughts and emotions as soon as you can. And you can do it right away, just by making the decision to accept what happened and let go of it.

Say the third Focus Phrase, "I accept everyone I work with, just as they are." This does not, of course, mean that you condone unacceptable behavior, or that you let others dominate you. It simply means that you are wise enough not to let other people determine your emotions and mood at work – or anywhere else, for that matter.

We all know someone who holds grudges for hours, sometimes for days, even for weeks. Those people poison their own moods and everyone else's. It's best not to let them provoke anger or resentment in you at all. If they do, use the third Focus Phrase to shift consciously back into acceptance.

As children, most of us learned that Jesus recommended we "love our enemies" and "do good to those who hurt us." At first, this seems irrational and unachievable at work. But when looked at from a more dispassionate psychological point of view, the advice is both rational and thoroughly achievable.

When we focus on acceptance and compassion, we feel good inside – and the world outside seems better too. Furthermore, chances are high that if we respond to someone's meanness with kindness, we'll help that person shift into a more positive mood.

THE NEED TO JUDGE

When we are at work, we are judging all the time. We have to evaluate ideas, plans, and strategies as part of our jobs. The problem arises when we come to evaluating other people. We tend to judge the people themselves rather than their ideas. We label people around us as "good" or "bad" or as "friendly" or unfriendly."

More often than not we apply negative judgments, which prevent us from being in more constructive states of mind. For the brain is wired in such a way that we can't simultaneously be busy

EMPATHY BOOST

judging, and feel compassion or expand into intuitive insight. They are incompatible mental states – you have to choose, each moment, which one to focus on.

Furthermore, we can't enjoy aesthetic and sensory pleasures until we take a breather from chronic judging and at least briefly accept the world just as it is. Judging also separates us from what we're experiencing. When we judge, we hold back and don't commit.

> Judgment, after all, is rooted in the fear function of the mind. We judge when we're apprehensive and suspect that something bad might happen if we aren't constantly careful. Conversely, we ease up and accept when we aren't afraid, when we can trust and open our hearts. So letting go of judgment is another way of letting go of anxiety.

Except for raw, visceral reactions, judgment is primarily a function of the thinking mind. We talk to ourselves when we judge. "I don't like my boss," or "The last time I spoke my mind in a meeting I got into trouble," or "I hate dealing with this customer." We all carry around a vast repertoire of judgmental one-liners that tend to run our lives – if we're not conscious of them. Almost constantly, as we look around us, we judge what we see, especially other people.

As long as you're caught up in judgment, you're not going to get very far in the process. You can't be creative, you can't be spontaneous, you can't serve your customers and support team spirit if you're regularly having thoughts that generate anxiety and distrust. With the third Uplift, you shift regularly out of judgment mode into its equal and opposite – that of accepting the world right now, just as it is, which includes accepting everyone you know, especially your coworkers, just as they are.

This doesn't mean you don't discriminate and be careful with people who can do you harm. It simply means that you accept the reality of how the world is in the present moment – because, indeed, to refuse to accept the world just as it is in the present moment is to fight against reality. And who can fight reality and win?

JUDGMENTAL EMOTIONS

Do you prefer to be judged or to be accepted? Do you value most a friend who unconditionally accepts you as you are or one who withholds real acceptance until you change in ways that they think you should? And at work, do you perform best on a team where there's mutual respect and acceptance, or where suspicion is constantly in the air?

When it comes right down to it, very little of a positive bent gets accomplished by spending a lot of valuable time judging the world around you. Just the opposite – you knock people down when you judge them. You close your heart when you're in judgment mode and cause defensive, even fearful reactions.

In our example from the beginning of the chapter, Ruth is sabotaging her career by judging others so much. Her first reaction to anyone on her team or beyond is to look for what is wrong with

EMPATHY BOOST

them. She is more concerned with seeming superior to her col-leagues than performing her work effectively and justifying her salary. Her judging creates anxiety, fear, and resentment of oth-ers, which saps Ruth's energy and the energy of those around her. She fritters away each day with corrosive gossip and complaining. Almost single-handedly, she has created a toxic work environ-ment in which she perceives everyone as a threat to her and reduces both the productivity and the mood of her team.

At the heart of judging is our desire to control the world by creating rules as to how others should think and behave. We then use these rules to evaluate other people, to label people as good or bad, smart or dumb, or friendly or hostile. Yet nobody can ever live up to such rules as they are often unrealistic, and they pre-vent us from seeing people as they really are with their unique mixtures of qualities and faults. Moreover, judging prevents us from accepting ourselves just as we are. We trap ourselves in an artificial reality of irrational and unworkable rules that hold us back from success and happiness.

So we need to break free of our rules and judgments and replace them with acceptance. For judging people traps them too, while acceptance helps to free them.

You know from your own experience that when your mind is in judgment mode, your heart tends to be cold and hard. When you shift into acceptance mode, all of a sudden there's a flow, you feel more open and empathic, and you relate better to your col-leagues.

Judgment wounds. Acceptance heals. Each time you move

through the Take Charge process you have the opportunity to replace mostly automatic judgment habits with feelings and perceptions based on acceptance. By this conscious act, you choose to accept everyone you encounter at work and offer them an uplift while maintaining your own. The third Take Charge step might seem quite quick and simple – but notice how it can transform your day.

JUST AS YOU ARE

Ruth had to learn acceptance, and she started by saying to herself, "I accept everyone at work, just as they are." She replaced her judgmental thoughts by pausing several times a day to say, "I accept everyone I know, just as they are." She did herself a great favor – freeing up the energy it took to maintain a negative thought against someone. She chose to shift from judgment mode into acceptance mode.

All of your coworkers are basically doing their best, caught up in their own programming and fears, hopes and struggles. Judging them doesn't improve the situation at all.

For her own benefit as well as that of her colleagues, Ruth said the Focus Phrases and began to develop empathy with everyone she met.

EMPATHY BOOST

GIVE YOURSELF TIME

The first time you say these words you might not notice any big changes. That's why we've structured the Take Charge process so that you return to the same focus again and again. Each new time that you say the words, you'll start to experience new thoughts and emotions.

For the first few days or weeks, as you say one of these statements and open up to whatever experience comes to you, don't immediately expect the world to shake. But at some point, suddenly the words are going to take on deeper meaning – and you'll feel the power that comes rushing in when you choose consciously to let go of judgments and consciously shine your light of acceptance and support on your fellow human beings.

As you'll learn in later chapters, there will be times when you reach this step in the process and a particular person will come to mind. In business or elsewhere, whenever you must relate with someone, the simple act of accepting them just as they are (even if they upset you) liberates you from all sorts of emotions that otherwise drag you down.

Acceptance sets you free – judgment continually limits you. As soon as you let go of your judgments toward a person, good things start to happen. As your perception changes, their response to you changes and the relationship improves. At work and equally at home, this third expansion can prove remarkably liberating.

Also, when you let go of judgment and tune into acceptance, you will find that your level of personal power suddenly surges. You naturally possess vastly more power than you probably realize or ever use. These Focus Phrases are designed to give you direct access to that power. It's your own power, after all, that activates your next breath. It's your own power that chooses to let go of your worries and accept the people around you.

Each time you move through the third step of the Take Charge process, you use this extraordinary power to transform your mood, your performance, and, above all, your relationships.

TAKE CHARGE UPLIFT 3:
FREE FROM JUDGMENT

Again, let's again talk you through what you've learned thus far, and then add the new Focus Phrase. Hold in mind that your main challenge is to move through this process over and over, until all you need to do is remember to say the Focus Phrases in turn – and the full Take Charge experience will happen effortlessly, and always in a new way.

EMPATHY BOOST

FROM JUDGMENT TO ACCEPTANCE!

Get comfortable . . . close your eyes if you want to . . . and when you're ready, say to yourself, "I give myself permission to feel good."

Exhale until you are empty of air . . . push with your stomach muscles to get all the air out . . . hold your breath on empty a moment . . . then relax as the new breath comes rushing into your lungs . . .

Tune into the feeling of the air flowing in your nose . . . and also the movements in your chest and belly as you breathe . . . and expand your awareness to include also the feelings in your heart . . . be aware of your whole body, here in this present moment . . . and expand to be aware also of the present-moment sounds . . . sights . . . scents . . .

Now say to yourself, "I let go of all my worries and feel peaceful in my mind." Be aware of how you feel in your head . . . relax the tensions in your scalp . . . your tongue and jaw . . . your eyes . . .

Breathe into the peace and quiet that you begin to feel in your head . . . and now you can say to yourself, "I accept everyone I work with, just as they are."

Allow this feeling of total acceptance and compassion to radiate out from your heart . . . surrender to the reality of the world just as it is . . . be open to a new experience!

PAUSE & EXPERIENCE

And now – here is the bare-bones short-form process, just the basic verbal cues that, once you memorize them, will instantly redirect your attention in directions that serve you remarkably well:

TAKE CHARGE – STEPS ONE, TWO, AND THREE

Say to yourself, "I give myself permission to feel good."
Exhale and hold your breath on empty.
Allow your inhalation to come on its own.
Feel the air flowing in and out of your nose.
Tune into the movements in your chest and belly.
Experience the feelings in your heart.
Be aware of your whole body in this present moment.
Tune into all your senses – and enjoy yourself!

Say "I let go of my worries and feel peaceful in my mind."
Allow peace to come!

Say "I accept everyone I know, just as they are."
Breathe . . . allow friendly feelings of empathy and team spirit to fill your heart . . . and open up to a new experience . . .

PAUSE & EXPERIENCE

EMPATHY BOOST

C H A P T E R 5

BOOST YOUR SELF-ESTEEM

CHAPTER 5: PREVIEW

Core Need – Boost Your Self-Esteem: Your self-esteem and optimism affect everything you do – self-esteem is the cornerstone of success. Your performance is determined by whether you feel positive about yourself – so you need to learn how to feel optimistic about the future, and also about your personal and professional self-worth in the present moment.

Our Solution: Our method helps you to eliminate ingrained negative attitudes and self-defeating thoughts which undermine your self-esteem and sabotage your career. We offer a daily process that begins to boost your sense of self-worth and confidence, as part of our Take Charge method.

The Process: Ultimately, you must choose to stop judging yourself negatively all the time and focus instead on accepting who you are and supporting your unique capabilities. This step of the Take Charge process will regularly help you accomplish the shift from self-negation to self-support.

Your Payoff: Employers reward employees who are self-confident and display high self-esteem – because these are winning qualities. By becoming your own best friend, you improve your chances for advancement. Your performance will shine, your sense of well-being and good health will improve, and you'll be more charismatic.

SELF-ESTEEM

DILEMMA AT WORK

Lorenzo is a brilliant economics professor. He is well respected at his university and has great leadership potential through his natural people skills and vision. But he has a fatal flaw he hasn't yet triumphed over – he carries around a negative image of himself and is constantly knocking himself down with his own attitudes. He is his own worst enemy because of this constant self-judgment and low self-image. This, in turn, has prevented him from being assertive in promoting his career. Not trusting or honoring his own potential, he avoids risk or projects where he believes he might fail. He stays in his comfort zone working behind the scenes with a few trusted colleagues, where he feels safe.

Lorenzo wants a promotion, yet he cannot bring himself to fight for it. He simply waits, hoping in vain that someone else will push and represent him instead. Through lack of acceptance and respect for his own self, he flounders. Fortunately Lorenzo does not need therapy or a major transformation to move forward. He can learn, right now, how to quiet negative thoughts that undermine his self-esteem and learn to accept himself just as he is. In the fourth step of the Take Charge method, he'll master powerful cognitive-shifting techniques that enable him to focus on his strengths and achieve his full potential. In short, he will consciously choose to access the inner resources he always has at his disposal and become his own best friend!

If you want to be a superb communicator, influence others,

and engender trust and confidence, then each day it's important to take time to nurture a good relationship with yourself. Unless you steadily expand your primary leadership qualities of emotional intelligence, self-awareness, and inner acceptance, chances are you're not operating at peak performance.

At first, you might find it self-indulgent or even narcissistic to focus on how you feel about yourself. But self-acceptance and a positive self-image are vital to your success at work and at home.

> Why is this true? Because a positive compassionate attitude toward yourself provides the essential emotional foundation for heightened mental clarity, creativity, empathy, and effective action.

We've been conditioned to believe that business is, by nature, a heartless, cutthroat activity in which hostility and aggression prevail over empathy, cooperation, and compassion. In fact, the opposite is true. Empathy and cooperation, not hostility and rivalry, are the hallmarks of a successful team. And emotional intelligence means knowing that how you feel toward yourself deep down determines how you relate with those around you.

Today we're able to discuss openly "emotional intelligence" as an essential characteristic of high-performing organizations. In this fourth Take Charge step, you will learn how to turn your focus directly to fostering empathy towards yourself. You'll see that it's actually bad for business if you do not accept and like

SELF-ESTEEM

yourself – because you will lack the confidence and power to be a truly dynamic team player and leader. Fostering self-esteem is not at all self-indulgent – it's the key to lasting success.

> You will increase your self-esteem, day by day, when you use the Take Charge program.

As an example: Lorenzo's colleague, Nicola, is less gifted academically than he is and has published far less. Yet she is now the senior professor, and this is because she has developed so much more confidence in herself. She is decisive, proactive, and self-assured. Her colleagues feel more comfortable around her, as she is comfortable in herself. They trust her leadership ability.

Indeed, effective leaders radiate confidence and empathy. They know that they must genuinely accept themselves just as they are, with no ifs, ands, or buts.

> You must learn to accept yourself unconditionally before you can accept others.

So ask yourself – do you honestly accept and respect yourself just as you are? Do you feel good in your heart about yourself – or do you carry around a negative judgmental attitude that you're not good enough or not smart enough, or that you're somehow too weak or ugly or foolish or otherwise unacceptable?

How do you see yourself – what are your negative one-liner

attitudes and judgments that continually knock you down and keep you from opening up and accepting yourself just as you are?

Take a few moments now to pause, perhaps put the book aside . . . tune into your breathing . . . and also the feelings in your heart . . . look within honestly, to see how you feel about yourself . . .

Do you like yourself . . . are you your own best friend . . . or do you judge yourself as somehow not lovable and okay just as you are? . . .

PAUSE & EXPERIENCE

YOUR OWN BEST FRIEND

We all want a best friend who likes and accepts us just as we are. That's what a best friend is all about, after all – a person we can just be ourselves with, and be accepted without judgment. We all hunger for this special relationship with a friend or lover in which we feel unconditionally accepted and cared for just as we are. Some people have been lucky enough to find such a best friend, but many people never do. Unconditional acceptance is, unfortunately, a rare commodity these days.

Here's our Take Charge solution to the dilemma: Instead of trying to find another person out there who is capable of accepting

SELF-ESTEEM

you just the way you are, why not just go ahead and become your own best friend? No one is stopping you from letting go of all your self-judgments and loving yourself just as you are. And the payoff is enormous.

> As soon as you decide to change from judging to accepting yourself, you unleash a unique power which can genuinely transform your life.

When you choose to be your own best friend, you choose to stop judging yourself and you also protect yourself from judgmental people.

In many years of working with private clients as well as in business settings, we've found that as soon as people choose to let go of negative childhood conditioning and accept themselves just as they are, a beautiful transformation begins to take place. Furthermore, when you accept yourself just as you are, you'll find that you become clearer in your thinking, possess more vitality, and manifest more creativity.

> Once there is a change of heart, all the rest unfolds naturally. So in practical terms, what can you do to encourage directly and regularly this deep shift from self-judgment to self-acceptance? How can you progress toward being your own best friend?

You probably already guessed the answer. On a daily or even hourly basis, begin to point your mind's all-powerful attention in the direction that nurtures self-acceptance by saying the Focus Phrases. Break out of old self-judgment habits by establishing positive self-acceptance habits that you practice regularly.

In other words, remember to move through the Take Charge process often each day so that you come to the fourth expansion. And when you get there, simply say to yourself, "I accept and love myself, just as I am." The words will turn your attention toward whatever acceptance and love you feel for yourself right then – and as you breathe into that positive feeling, it will expand (and self-judgment will decrease more and more).

Of course, this takes time, but each time you move through the process, you'll find that something happens, your heart opens up to yourself a little more – and this always feels great!

Over time, you will boost your self-esteem by practicing this focus phrase. You will gain more confidence and charisma at work as you learn to rise above any negative conditioning.

WHAT LORENZO LEARNED

For several weeks, Lorenzo has diligently studied and begun to master the Take Charge method. Today he's at a faculty meeting and is due to give a presentation in just a few minutes. He's nervously awaiting his turn to speak. As the moments tick by, he becomes more tense and worried as his mind spins negative one-liners about how he might stumble and fail.

His emotions naturally react to his lack of self-confidence by

SELF-ESTEEM

making him feel weak and shaky. His breathing becomes tight and shallow, his consciousness contracts – he has become a victim of his inner insecurities and lost the confidence in himself that he so desperately needs in order to communicate well and impress his peers.

How can Lorenzo break free of this worried, depressed state of mind and body and quickly shift his state of mind so that he may give a great presentation?

The answer is for him to move quickly through the Take Charge process. If you're in a similar situation, the answer will be the same for you. Here are your guidelines for regaining your self-esteem when you lose it:

One: First of all, realize that apprehensions and negative thoughts have taken over your mind – your breathing is tense and shallow, your body weak with worry, and your heart contracted and numb.

Seeing this dilemma, start talking to yourself. Exhale and say, "I give myself permission to feel good." Hold on empty until you shift away from thoughts and feel that positive spark of life in your solar plexus. Then relax and allow that next good inhalation to come rushing in – enjoy the air rushing in through your nose, the expansion in your chest and belly, and your emergence into whole-body awareness.

Two: Especially if time is short, just moving through that first step can do the trick. You'll break free from inner torments, tune in to your core power and the feelings in your heart, and feel much better. If you have a bit more time, however, you'll want to move right into the second expansion and say to yourself, "I let go of my worries and feel peaceful in my mind." Allow these words to set your breathing even more free and bring a good feeling of mental calm into your head.

Three: If time allows, you can now move into the third expansion by saying, "I accept everyone here, just as they are." Let go of your negative judgment of the people you're going to talk to, set your heart free of the burden of tension between you and people around you. Choose to accept the world just as it is – because that moves you into an optimum position of inner clarity and power.

Four: Once you've advanced to this point in the Take Charge process, you can go the next crucial step. Say to yourself the magic words that most powerfully activate self-esteem and confidence: "I accept myself, just as I am."

As his time comes to stand and talk in front of the group, Lorenzo can now do so with full-body charisma, radiating good feelings, meeting people's glances with acceptance and compassion. His mind is again sharp, his senses alert, and his heart open to cooperation and win-win communication.

That's the basic success formula – and following that is the Emergency Uplift in short form, for basic practice and memorization. Hold in mind that each time you walk yourself through the process, allowing the statements to reverberate throughout your being, you'll get better at this process.

SELF-ESTEEM

Definitely, practice makes perfect – so give yourself at least five to ten short breathers during each of the following days to master this process and truly learn it by heart. When you're put on hold anytime, anywhere in the next weeks, instead of sitting there twiddling your thumbs or feeling bored or impatient, remember to do your Take Charge homework and walk through the process you're learning here.

Every time you do this, you'll benefit immediately by raising your spirits, and you'll also exercise that mental muscle for taking charge of your moods and mind states and actively shifting into higher realms of performance and well-being.

EMERGENCY UPLIFT

"I give myself permission to feel good."

Exhale – hold – inhale – come alive!

"I let go of my worries and feel peaceful in my mind."

"I accept everyone I know, just as they are."

"I accept and love myself, just as I am."

Head into action – with confidence and power!

INCREMENTAL PROGRESS

When you say, "I accept myself, just as I am," and let the words reverberate throughout your being, something *will* happen if you're conscious of your breathing and feelings.

In the beginning, you might find that your mind reacts with words such as "No, that's not true, I don't accept myself just as I am, I'm a wreck!" If this happens, all you need to do is say the words again and allow them to point your mind's attention toward whatever compassion you do feel for yourself – even if it's just a little bit. The intent is to get your attention aimed at the compassion, and away from the judgment.

What you'll discover, even if you only find a tiny bit of love and acceptance for yourself in your heart and mind, is that when your loving attention (stimulated by the words of the Focus Phrase) is aimed at your heart, good feelings are awakened.

And this feeling of feeling your heart contracted and then experiencing it opening just a tiny bit is absolutely wonderful. This is where the good feelings are to be found – so experiment with opening to the feeling of accepting yourself just as you are. For just a few breaths at a time, risk seeing what happens when you stop judging yourself and become your own best friend. We assure you that nothing bad is going to happen if you ease up on yourself.

SELF-ESTEEM

"I accept and love myself just as I am." Please note that the power of these words on their own is not as great as when you say them after moving through the first three steps of the Take Charge process, because the experience of opening up to loving yourself more fully happens best when you're focused fully in the present moment, when your level of anxiety and worry has been calmed, and when your judgmental thoughts about the world and other people are quiet. Then, when you have prepared yourself with the first three expansions, you are ready to take the next giant step – that of opening your heart into a new sense of accepting yourself unconditionally.

We all know that, in raising children, if we constantly withhold love and instead criticize and point out all their negative qualities, their spirit and performance wither. If we regularly tell children that we love and support them and focus on their positive qualities, they blossom. All we're suggesting here is that you start treating yourself as a loved child – give yourself more and more acceptance on a regular basis and you'll blossom.

As you approach this expansive Take Charge experience (which is always going to be a new experience), you don't need to think about the meaning of the words you say, just experience saying them to yourself, and let them resonate . . . move through all four together now, devoting a breath or two or three to each . . . and feel how they function as a team:

"I give myself permission to feel good."
"I let go of my worries and feel peaceful in my mind."
"I accept the world, just as it is."
"I accept, love, and honor myself just as I am."

PAUSE & EXPERIENCE

"TAKE CHARGE" IN ACTION

For your own sake, please learn these four Focus Phrases by heart as soon as you can, even as we add more phrases in the next few chapters. There are only three more phrases – we're almost to the end of learning the process. Memorization does take a little effort, but you'll find the energy expended well worth it. As mentioned before, if you want audio guidance, feel free to go online to http://takechargetraining.com and allow our voices to guide you effortlessly through the process, enough times to where all this becomes second nature.

SELF-ESTEEM

What's important in this process is allowing these key words that you speak to actually touch your heart and mind as they resonate deeper and deeper. Each of the primary Focus Phrases is a psychological doorway that lets you experience directly and immediately more and more of who you really are.

In the process of discovering who you really are, you'll tap powers of creativity, charisma, and leadership that accelerate your rise to the top of your chosen profession or work. Our job here is to show you the door – yours is to walk regularly through that door.

TAKE CHARGE SALES STRATEGY

When we enjoy high self-esteem we greatly improve our performance at work, and nowhere is this more true than in sales. Less experienced as well as less successful salespeople tend to be insecure in sales calls and compensate by relying on scripts and tricks to manipulate the customer. Psychologically, manipulation is a fear-based action of the ego where, rather than trusting himself or the customer, the salesperson is trying to exert control through clever words or strategies.

Imagine the case of an office equipment salesperson presenting a range of copiers to a new customer. He can approach this customer either in a controlling, untrusting way, with the intent of playing a game to manipulate this person into a sale – or he can trust himself to be friendly and spontaneous and approach the customer with the intent of discovering his needs, being responsive, and closing the sale if it is appropriate.

The manipulative salesperson regards the customer as a "means" to satisfy his selfish "ends." If he is good at such manipulative sales, he knows how to play on the person's weaknesses and lead him to buy the copier he wants to sell – even if that's not what the customer really wants. The salesperson stays locked into thinking mode and ignores his feelings and the feelings of the customer.

On the other hand, the experienced, successful salesperson who enjoys high self-esteem chooses to feel good about herself, enjoy the moment, and participate in helping customers find what they want – or accepting that they don't have what the customers want.

This top salesperson's self-esteem is not dependent on whether she closes the sale or not. It is a much more secure and resilient self-esteem which is always present, irrespective of the outcome of the call. She is her own best friend and does not act from fear. Instead, she says to herself, "I let go of my worries (of not getting a sale) and feel peaceful in my mind." In turn, the customer sees that this salesperson is calm, not worried, and confident – and he responds in kind. The top salesperson creates trust and good feelings in everyone she meets.

Also, rather than judging the customer, this salesperson can say to himself, "I accept this person just as he/she is," which allows him to approach the customer with a feeling of empathy

SELF-ESTEEM

rather than judgment. This wakes up a radiant presence inside, leading to genuine rapport with the customer.

In this expanded state of empathy and self-acceptance, the top salesperson will enjoy the present moment and listen to the customer's needs without any manipulative scheming, and the customer will feel acknowledged and valued. The very experience of spending time with this person will be a positive event for both of them, whether or not a sale is concluded. The salesperson will only sell to the customer if he has the right solution. Otherwise, he might recommend another supplier, as he knows that building a long-term relationship on trust is more important than going for the instant gratification of an inappropriate sale.

This "participatory rather than manipulative" approach to business is becoming more popular – because it works. By honoring your inner feelings, you stay friendly and responsive. And by redirecting attention from what you want to what the customer wants, you increase sales. Both you and the customer benefit from the experience.

In the Take Charge approach, the sales process becomes more than a business transaction. It becomes an opportunity to help each other and build a genuine relationship. In each and every situation you enter at work, you have the choice of practicing the

Take Charge process. You can choose to focus on empathy and service or lock into manipulative behavior and mind states that might serve your short-term desires, but in the long term come back to haunt you.

HOLD THAT THOUGHT

Another aspect of self-acceptance and enhanced esteem that we should mention has to do with the universal mental habit of running a particular negative thought or phrase through your mind, repeating it subliminally over and over.

Everyone sometimes finds himself fixated on vague thoughts such as "I know I'm going to be late with this report," or "I'm just too dumb for this job," or "I'm really tired of that guy," or "I wish I were on vacation," or "If I mess up, they're going to fire me," or "Nobody here really likes me," or some similar negative thought. Without conscious mind management, such vague irritating thoughts run out of control and pollute the whole day.

What can you do to override such habitual thought-flows? Our Take Charge strategy suggests that you use this same repetition mechanism to your positive advantage, by developing the habit of running more useful, effective thoughts in your awareness – specifically, the Focus Phrases we're teaching you.

We mentioned earlier that it's a good idea to move through the full set of Focus Phrases we're teaching you, together and in proper order. This is certainly true when you are doing them as a unified process, as a whole experience. But after you've moved through the full process at least once (early in the day is optimal),

SELF-ESTEEM

please feel free then to allow one or more of the Focus Phrases to stay with you, as a constant, quiet reminder that fills that part of your mind where your negative one-liners usually lurk.

Imagine how good and relaxed you would feel if you regularly held in mind the sentences "I'm aware of the feelings in my heart" and "I give myself permission to feel good." Or you might choose to stop feeling anxious by remembering the phrase "I let all my worries go." And always recall the primary focus phrase "I love myself just as I am."

TAKE CHARGE UPLIFT 4:

BE YOUR OWN BEST FRIEND

Again, move calmly into full awareness of . . .

. . . your breathing . . .

. . . your heart . . .

. . . your whole-body presence . . .

. . . and now advance through the following Focus Phrases.

Let them do their magic . . . give them time to touch your heart . . .

"I give myself permission to feel good."

. . . be open to a new experience.

"I let go of my worries and feel peaceful in my mind."

. . . be open to a new experience.

"I accept everyone I know, just as they are."

. . . be open to a new experience.

"I accept and love myself, just as I am."

. . . be open to a new experience.

PAUSE & EXPERIENCE

SELF-ESTEEM

PART THREE

Insight, Wisdom, and Integrity

Rule your mind
Or it will rule you.
- Horace

CHAPTER 6

STIMULATE CREATIVE BREAKTHROUGHS

GET CREATIVE

CHAPTER 6: PREVIEW

Core Need – Think More Creatively: You need to be creative to ensure the competitiveness of your organization. You should be able to generate new ideas, plus seek and discover new customer needs and solutions. Yet often when faced with problems large or small, you might tend to get stuck in routine thinking patterns. You can now consciously act to enhance your creativity by shifting into full-brain integration.

Our Solution: Your mind has five different areas of performance – and only when you learn how to integrate all these functions into creative flashes of insight, do you tap your full creative potential. Our Take Charge method leads you, step by step, to the point where this flash of creativity occurs.

The Process: Each of our Focus Phrases points your attention deeper and deeper toward your creative spark of genius. When you pause and take charge of your mind for just a few minutes, you can actively shift into creative mode.

Your Payoff: In all areas of your life, mastering the core skill of creativity activation will spark success and fulfillment. Both with minor challenges and with the larger issues facing the world, you can make a difference by expanding your perspective to see the greater whole and opening up to receive insights from your full-brain potential.

DILEMMA AT WORK

Vanessa is a customer-service representative for a high-growth software corporation in California. She is a great plotter and planner, but she seems to lack the creative spark that generates new ideas and insights at work. She plays by the rules and follows and finds it difficult to break out of her programmed responses to customer problems. So instead of fulfilling her creative potential, she remains unhappily stuck in positions for which she is overqualified. Her problem is clear: She doesn't know how to manage her mind so that she shifts regularly into more creative and intuitive modes of thinking.

Her solution is to learn how to break out of her comfort zone and temporarily silence routine thoughts based on what's worked in the past. Only then will she be able to receive flashes of insight and brilliance from her more creative mental faculties. She needs to master the Take Charge process that immediately turns her mind's focus away from the old, toward the new.

You must let go of the old to create space for the new, if you want to advance in the constantly changing and challenging world of work. You are always being required to replace old knowledge and techniques with new ones. Yet the most important change you need to make is not replacing old information – it is replacing old ways of using your mind. To advance and be creative you must momentarily quiet the mind and let go of the constant murmur of thoughts in your head, if you want to

GET CREATIVE

open up to receive insights from the deeper creative potential of your mind.

You know the feeling of jamming hard to solve a frustrating dilemma at work, frying your brain with every logical angle you can think of, but still not coming up with a creative answer. The truth is, many problems cannot be solved just by applying past logic and routine strategies.

> Many work dilemmas require a leap of insight and creativity. Let go of your programmed responses to problems, take a breather, step back and with a fresh mind, take a new perspective and see the big picture.

Only when you choose to make this cognitive shift do you expand your mind's functioning beyond old habits and discover new inspirations that solve the dilemma. We all want to know how to accomplish this shift from routine mental problem-solving into creative insight. And the Take Charge process offers the exact step-by-step approach to becoming creative at work.

The first step is to realize that you're not making progress with your old approach and that you're burned out from pushing with your regular problem-solving techniques. You need to admit that your usual tools aren't getting the job done – and decide instead to use our five-step process that will shift your mind into higher gear.

So – you take a breather and say to yourself, "I give myself permission to feel good," and move through that initial process – because flashes of insight don't emerge when you're tense and out of touch with good feelings in your body. They emerge when you ease up and give yourself permission to enjoy the present moment.

The creative mind also requires at least a temporary abeyance of worries and the stress of anxiety. A worried mind is contracted and seriously uncreative – so you move right on and say, "I let go of my worries and feel peaceful in my mind."

This essential step frees up your mind – it's the act of letting go that creates space for something new to emerge. Very often, when we encounter a problem at work, we tense up with a worried reaction to the dilemma, so it's best to deal with the anxiety before trying to solve the problem.

The third requirement of a creative mind is to put aside temporarily its judging bias that is always ready to criticize whatever new insights you might come up with. Creative problem-solving requires taking chances, risking unsuccessful attempts, venturing beyond the tried-and-tested into new perspectives. If you're afraid of being laughed at, especially by your own judgmental self, it's time to let go of judgments so that you're free to create.

For this specific problem-solving application of the Take Charge process, you can modify the "I accept everyone at work, just as they are," and say instead, "I let go of being critical – I let go of judging." At least for a few minutes, suspend the critical edge of your mind, so that you can entertain new possibilities and explore flashes of unexpected insight.

GET CREATIVE

Furthermore, if you're not feeling good about yourself, you will sabotage your own creativity. There's nothing that ruins the insight process more than being judgmental toward yourself. As long as you allow old self-defeating attitudes to dominate your mind, with one-liners such as "I'm not creative," or "I never come up with good ideas," or "I'm no good at these things," your creative potential is kept at a minimum.

It's always wise to devote just a breath or two to activating your "best friend" relationship with yourself by saying, "I accept and love myself just as I am."

> Creativity requires a lightness of being, a sense of acceptance, and openness to trust and risk. Awaken your ability to relax, enjoy, expand – and then tap your spontaneous wellsprings of inventiveness and inspiration.

RECEIVING FULL-BRAIN FLASHES

Through a minute or two of inner preparation for creative problem-solving, you shift your consciousness to where you're ready to access insight via full-brain integration. Then say to yourself your specific intent: "I am ready to receive insight into my dilemma." Say it – do it! Shift into receive mode in your mind. Become receptive to insight.

Creativity cannot be provoked or pushed into action – but it can be given space and allowed to happen. This conscious act of moving through the first four expansions and then saying, "I am ready to receive insight into my dilemma," is the most direct path we've found for instantly overriding all the limitations, confusions, compulsions, worries, and fixations of your everyday mind and shifting into more creative action.

As practice in shifting into creative mode at work, again move through the four preparatory steps you are learning. Say: "I give myself permission to feel good . . . I let go of my worries and feel peaceful in my mind . . . I let go of being judgmental . . . I love myself just as I am."

When you're ready, say to yourself several times on your exhalations, "I am open to receive insight."

In the next few moments, continue to stay aware of your breathing . . . your heart . . . your whole-body presence . . . and make friends with this "open to receive" state of mind . . . set your awareness free to explore whatever new ideas, new visions, and new approaches might come spontaneously to mind . . .

PAUSE & EXPERIENCE

GET CREATIVE

SCIENCE AND BEYOND

As we move into this fifth expansion, we enter the zone where our scientific understanding of the brain and consciousness reaches its known limits. Scientists are the first to admit that they don't know much at all about how our consciousness functions when it comes to creativity and intuitive flashes.

The intuitive function of the mind remains a great mystery. We know that the brain can shift into higher gear and deliver an integrated experience of "knowing" that lies beyond deductive reasoning altogether. But we don't know scientifically how this actually happens inside the brain.

What we do know from brain-scan research is that we tend to use a limited portion of our mind when deductively thinking about something, but when we become momentarily quiet and then have flashes of insight that pop suddenly into the mind, a much larger portion of the brain is being used during those flashes, including not just the left-brain reasoning areas, but also the right-brain creative regions.

Businesspeople are generally happier staying firmly in the realm of deductive logic. They rightly want to support their decision-making with empirical evidence and quantifiable data. Then they can reduce the risk of making a poor decision and also clearly explain and justify their reasoning. They are less comfortable with this mysterious function of intuition and insight.

This type of total-brain "inspired" mental activity
is not yet taught in business schools, nor
adequately compensated in budgets. Yet it is
unquestionably clear that competitive organizations
need to be constantly innovative – and innovation
requires steady doses of intuition and insight.

Once you learn to access your creative potential you will notice that you see things differently. As with a camera, you can move your focus from a tight "telephoto lens" view, where you zoom in on a specific feature of your problem, to a "wide angle" view, where you see the whole problem in context, and perceive the broader picture. From this broader "all at once" view you can recognize connections and patterns that were not visible with your telephoto view and through this new perspective facilitate creative breakthroughs.

As Vanessa learned how to take charge of her mind, she was able to discover her wide-angle lens – and she could think more creatively about customer service. She could step back and see her work from different perspectives. She began learning how other businesses approached the issues she faced day to day – and moved from being a routine problem-solver to being a creative consultant for her customers. She not only fixed their

GET CREATIVE

stated problems but added value by helping her customers improve their overall systems and processes.

Vanessa changed the way she used her mind. She expanded her thinking beyond old assumptions and routines, and thus learned to break out of her box. For many years she had been encouraged by her boss to do just that – to "think outside the box." But part of her problem was that she was literally stuck in a box of her corporation's own making. Like millions of others, Vanessa worked in a small cubicle in a large office of scores of similar cubicles. Her office environment was hardly conducive to creativity. Every week or so she was invited to a "brainstorming" meeting in a bigger cubicle, where she was supposed to blossom into a Leonardo da Vinci for two hours or so. But until she learned the Take Charge process, she had no idea how to shift into the right state of mind to access insights and moments of brilliance. Once she learned how to take charge of her mind, she could create her own inner creative landscape of peace and calm. She became more relaxed and confident, and knew how to enter into "the zone" where her creative juices could flow freely – she turned a big corner in her career.

Probably, in your own situation, your work conditions are not all that conducive to the kind of creative thinking you're expected to deliver. Now you can create an inner environment that fosters and supports creativity – so you become creative more often and more successfully.

DELAYED EFFECT ~ HIGH IMPACT

There's nothing that turns off intuition more than impatience and, likewise, there's no way to push insight into being. You can only allow it to come to you at its own good speed. You might search for answers to dilemmas and sometimes wait weeks – whereas at other times, even before you get through the first four expansions, pow! Suddenly, the answer flashes in full bloom into your mind.

With the first four Take Charge steps, the intent and the pay-off are immediate. You tune in to the air flowing in and out of your nose and almost instantly your breathing deepens, and as your awareness expands into whole-heart, whole-body awareness, good feelings brighten the present moment.

You then say to yourself, "I let go of my worries and feel peaceful in my mind," and (once you get good at it) you feel the effects immediately. Same with letting go of judgment and loving yourself – say it, and right away there's almost always a positive response.

You move through the full process and most definitely attain an inner sense of calm and pleasure right away, as you become relaxed, more centered, joyful, and powerful. But then as you contemplate your dilemma, perhaps moments go by, then min-utes – and often you end the reflection session with no solution yet in hand.

What do you do? You let go of immediate payoff, move on to other things, and purposefully allow the creative process to shift into incubation mode.

GET CREATIVE

When you enter into the depths of the Take Charge experience, you put into motion inner ruminations and connections that often take time to manifest as something specific. Only after you get out and engaged again with your everyday routines do certain insights tend to rise to the surface and manifest as actual noticeable thoughts and actions.

This is the "delayed effect" that we're encouraging you to be patient with, as insights and guidance work their way, in their own good time, to the surface of your awareness. And how do they tend to appear? Sometimes they come as a sudden clear thought, as a complete answer to your dilemma. At other times, an insight can manifest as a slowly dawning realization that grows until you become aware of its existence in your mind. Sometimes you might have a dream that stimulates the insight, or something you hear someone say sparks the answer. Some people talk of hearing their inner voice speaking to them.

The insight you seek can come in many ways. But when it comes, you usually recognize it immediately as a valuable flash of realization and understanding. You can't always say where it came from or how it came to you, but you have it! This is our goal here – and your challenge is to practice with the process until it comes alive for you.

TAKE CHARGE UPLIFT 5:
ENCOURAGING CREATIVE THINKING

Wherever you are – at work, at home, or anywhere else – there is nothing stopping you from saying the following sentences to yourself – and shifting into a more creative, insightful state of mind.

Move calmly into full awareness of your breathing . . . your heart . . . your whole-body presence . . . and then advance through the following Focus Phrases. Let them do their magic . . . give them time to touch your heart.

"I give myself permission to feel good." Experience this . . .

"I let go of my worries and feel peaceful in my mind." Experience this . . .

"I accept everyone I know, just as they are." Experience this . . .

"I love myself just as I am." Experience this . . .

"I am open to receive insight into my dilemma."

Don't do anything now . . . just stay aware of yourself breathing in the present moment . . . enjoy being here . . . and at the same time, allow your awareness to expand to include the dilemma you're seeking to resolve . . . just breathe into the presence of this dilemma . . . accept it . . . and while your breaths come and go . . . be open to a new experience . . .

PAUSE & EXPERIENCE

GET CREATIVE

And now let's see how you're doing with memorizing, learning by heart, these five Take Charge Focus Phrases.

After reading this paragraph, see what happens when you close your eyes and let your ego voice remember and say to yourself each of the five Focus Phrases several times, one after the other . . . enjoy the pure pleasure of saying these statements . . . allow each statement of intent to resonate throughout your being . . .

PAUSE & EXPERIENCE

CHAPTER 7

GENERATE TRUSTWORTHY DECISIONS

CHAPTER 7: PREVIEW

Core Need – Think Strategically: You have to be able to think and act strategically to advance your career. Organizations need people who can see the big picture and move forward with a long-term vision. There is a premium on proactivity, confidence in action, and wisdom in leadership.

Our Solution: The capacity for strategic thinking is a skill that can be greatly augmented if you use the correct mind-management tools. Our method advances through five key preparations each time you move through the process, so that you arrive at a quality of consciousness that encourages flashes of a greater vision and confidence that the greater vision is good and right.

The Process: By the time you arrive at this sixth expansion, your mind is quiet, free from worries and distractions, and plugged in to your higher intuitive function. As you maintain this special quality of consciousness, you are in the optimum position to perceive the whole of a situation and tune in to insights that are strategically powerful and reflect your total intelligence and wisdom. You learn to move beyond your preferred mode of thinking and apply and integrate multiple modes. This gives you a far more elegant and effective understanding and greatly enhances your decision-making capability. We call this process "five-star intelligence."

Your Payoff: As you develop this skill for regularly expanding your perspective into five-star intelligence and full-brain vision, your value in your organization will rise rapidly – especially as you make and implement better decisions and enhance your leadership capacity.

DILEMMA AT WORK

Tom is now chief financial officer at an exciting biotech corporation. He's just taken up his position in San Diego and has all the qualities, except for one, to be CEO someday. The quality he currently lacks is the ready ability to access high-level strategic thinking – the key attribute of a successful CEO. He's a master of detail and has a natural affinity for data and logical problem-solving. This has helped him succeed at college and, up to now, in his work. However his strong preference for logic is providing diminishing returns. For Tom has never developed the ability to step back and see the whole. He also has trouble envisioning the future, gaining a deep "feel" for a situation, and making inspired strategic decisions. Indeed, he assumes that strategic thinking is an ability you either "have or don't have" – and he thinks he just doesn't have it.

Tom needs to let go of his defeatist attitude about not being able to think strategically and make wise decisions. Then he needs to practice with regularity the Take Charge process for shifting into an expanded state of mind where he can see the whole at once, tap "five-star intelligence" – and gain that powerful perspective from which wise, powerful, and successful decisions emerge.

In the "Wake Up/Feel Good" first step of the Take Charge process, you dealt with the physical dimensions of superior performance at work – the basic process of quite literally coming to your senses and waking up to your whole-body presence in the here and now. In steps two, three, and four, you turned to your emotions, your judgments, and your relationship with yourself. With step five, you took a major step deeper into your inner potential, looking to activate your creative insight.

Now it's time, in this sixth expansion, to integrate and activate all five dimensions of consciousness at once, to help awaken advanced strategic thinking or what is often called wisdom – that inner source of truly trustworthy decisions and business action.

> You are able to develop your own integrated capacity
> for wise decision-making and leadership. It is not a
> mysterious gift you are born with.

Our media culture is steeped in images of wise people from our history, including political leaders like George Washington, Thomas Jefferson, Abraham Lincoln, and Martin Luther King Jr., plus Native American leaders such as Chief Joseph and Cochise, and service leaders such as Saint Teresa.

But what do we really mean by wisdom, particularly in the workplace? It is often sought after, much admired, and trusted – but few people have attempted to explore practically what makes a person wise and how we can purposefully increase our wisdom. This chapter details a new method for becoming more wise – one that all of us can readily participate in.

OUR NATURAL CONDITION

We are able to act more wisely when we choose to manage our minds in such a way as to expand into full-brain and whole-body awareness – and speak up and act from this grounded core of being.

> Wisdom is when we move beyond our normal modes of thought and stop judging our colleagues, and start to see the bigger picture. Wisdom comes into being when we pause to consider all the experiences and data we've accumulated related to a situation and then shift into intuitive mode to integrate the information and experience into a deeper sense of "knowing" and inner clarity.

Wisdom is about moving beyond our comfort zone. In our example, Tom needs to make wiser decisions as CFO. A vital part of his job is to make acquisitions, yet he has regularly turned down opportunities because he has been stuck in a short-term, fear-based mode of thought.

Now when Tom considers potential acquisitions, he will be able to think at a deeper level and make a far wiser decision than he has before.

First, he will move beyond the immediate data, and see the bigger picture beyond the numbers. He will use new ways of thinking strategically and consult with innovative and creative thinkers, rather than just relying on his own judgment as he has before. Previously, he had seen consulting with others as a sign of weakness. Now he has the wisdom to seek out help.

The more Tom lets go of his old, narrow analytical approach, the more he can see opportunities that the acquisition presents. He might have rejected it before, but now he can see beyond the short-term consequences to the long-term potential.

Previously, Tom had been motivated by the fear of loss, the fear of making a mistake, which had led to his organization missing out on some great deals. Now he acts without fear and, using his wisdom, thinks about what his employer has to gain – not what he has to lose.

Tom was able to expand his awareness to use his intuition and his feelings to achieve a deeper understanding and make a wiser decision. The next Focus Phrase enables you to do the same when you say to yourself "I feel connected with my inner source of wisdom."

WITHOUT . . . WITHIN

If you observe where you usually aim your attention at work, you'll find that it's mostly aimed outward. Our culture programs us to fixate on externals, rather than to look within to observe our own integrated mental functioning. Our education system forces children to acquire knowledge and concepts without being aware of *how* they actually think. We receive no training at all in most of our schools in the basic mind management you're learning here.

For instance, unless you were unusually blessed, no teacher ever encouraged you to turn your attention regularly to your own inner experience – your heart, your breathing, your whole-body presence.

> Your high-school curriculum was devoid of concrete training related to accessing intuitive insight and perspective. And certainly, nobody showed you the great value of aiming your awareness regularly toward your own inner integrative process.

Instead, your mind's focus was required to remain externally fixated – on textbooks, on teachers talking nonstop at you, on events and presentations, and on the constant drone of repetition and abstract data-gathering.

And when you graduated from high school or college and moved on to your first job, nothing changed. If anything, work proved even more externally fixated. You were told to trust only quantifiable data, not more subtle perceptions, thoughts, and insights that emerged from your full-brain deeper source of knowing. Therefore, it's to be assumed that you have had very little training in purposefully aiming your attention inward toward your personal source of wisdom.

We know from experience that insight and
certainty emerge from our inner core of intelligence.
Wisdom comes from within. But turning our mind's
focus 180 degrees, from external fixation to internal
fixation, is still considered a radical mental act.

Therefore we've created the Take Charge process, which very gently leads you through the "look within" experience over and over – until you begin to develop a strong mental muscle for turning your attention toward your own source of wisdom.

THE SEVEN WISDOM QUALITIES

At this point in our discussion, we're ready to identify the seven primary aspects of wisdom.

Wisdom Quality ~ One

Wise individuals tend to *be grounded in their own bodies,* experientially aware, tuned in to the present moment, and connected with the world. They are perceptually sharp and spontaneously responsive to everything happening around them. Charismatic leaders naturally enjoy these qualities and inspire and motivate us with their very presence, without the use of manipulation or quick fixes. They are completely authentic, not trying to be someone else or prove anything.

This is authentic wise leadership. Imagine how you would shine at work if you chose to focus more intently and regularly on your own dynamic physical presence.

Wisdom Quality ~ Two

Wise people tend to be *less fearful.* They have learned to release worries and anxiety. Most of us have one or more fears which hold us back. For some it is a fear of not being recognized or approved; for others it is a fear of change or losing control; for many it is a fear of rejection, an insecurity that we will be exposed as incompetent and unworthy. Wise people rise above these fears and see reality clearly, not distorted by their fears and anxieties. This quality of consciousness includes a special *quietness of mind* that allows for inner reflection and clear observation of reality. Wise people are not as lost in their own thoughts – and this also makes them good listeners.

Consider how much more effective you could be at work if you acted with less anxiety and more acceptance of reality. Then you could make decisions based on what is right, not on what is the easiest and safest.

Wisdom Quality ~ Three

Wise people are *not judgmental.* Their wisdom comes from a quality of consciousness that perceives reality without prejudice, and therefore sees a situation clearly. When we are in the presence of a wise person, we feel that we are seen for who we really are, and respected and supported without being stereotyped. From this nonjudgmental perspective, a wise person can look to see the truth of the matter, free from past assumptions. Leaders with this quality boost the confidence and self-esteem of everyone around them. This is fundamental to a positive work culture.

> How would people respond to you if you judged them less, accepted them more – and therefore encouraged empathy at work and regularly perceived your various challenges with more clarity and insight?

Wisdom Quality ~ Four

Wise people feel more *compassionate and connected.* At this level, people often talk about "thinking and acting from the heart" as a key quality of wisdom. Wise leaders have learned how to integrate their cognitive experience in the head with their emotional experience in the heart. Their perceptions and decisions are therefore more profound and generally more accurate. This leads to superior performance in all areas of work.

Imagine if you were able to see the best in your
colleagues at work and feel a deep sense of
connection and empathy for them.
Imagine if all of your team did the same.

Wisdom Quality ~ Five

Wise people know how to shift from the tightness of their
habitual thinking mind into that *open-to-receive* state of consciousness, in which insights and inspiration can flash into being
from their total-brain experience. They readily move into this
heightened level of creativity when they encounter a challenge at
work and flash with new ideas that are both reliable and inspired.

Imagine yourself regularly choosing to shift into the
quality of mind in which you access your own greater
intuitive functions, and thus become the one at work
with insights that are respected and employed.

Wisdom Quality ~ Six

Wise leaders either spontaneously or through concerted inner
training know how to make the final expansion of their mental performance so that all *five dimensions of consciousness* are activated
at once. They know how to orchestrate their own consciousness so

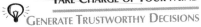
that a full integration occurs between heart, mind, and body, generating predictably wise decisions, whereas most of us tend to stay in our secure preferred mode of thinking, whether it be sticking to routine, working mostly with data, or remaining inside safe ideas. Wise people integrate all modes so they can expand their thinking to a far broader and more profound level.

Imagine being able to harness the great power of wisdom within your own consciousness so that you regularly shift into the true state of "knowing" at work – and express your vision clearly and fearlessly.

Wisdom Quality ~ Seven

Finally – wise leaders *know when to act* and when not to act. They might sometimes seem quiet and reflective, yet they can shift into powerful action when needed. They are decisive and not afraid of making difficult decisions, which they wholeheartedly follow through to completion. In business terms they know how to "execute," how to get things done – especially the difficult tasks that need completion.

Imagine developing your capacity to know when you are right, and then having the courage to act on your decisions – with certainty and integrity.

NATURE PLUS NURTURE

As you can clearly see, these seven primary qualities of wisdom are exactly the same qualities that we are learning to develop in the Take Charge process.

> We've designed the Take Charge system so that everything you do here aims you toward accessing and then expanding your innate capacity for wise leadership.

In this sixth step of the full Take Charge process, you aim all your attention toward the ultimate goal of integrating everything that has come before – so you can actively tap your ever-evolving capacity to know from the depths of your heart and soul what is right to do in any particular situation.

We hope you are now beginning to sense the wholeness and, indeed, the wisdom of this seven-step process. Certainly, there will be many times when you don't move through all seven steps – you might be struggling with a problem at work and pause to go through just the five steps that lead to opening to intuitive insight into your problem.

Leading your mind into this stage of openness to insight will serve you beautifully. But we also encourage you, at least a few times a day, not to stop with the fifth step – but to move on through the sixth and seventh steps.

All of us have an inherent capacity for spontaneous
wisdom. And by regularly moving through the sixth and
seventh steps of this program, you will be led deeper
and deeper into tapping your true potential and power.

Nature, of course, does have something to do with our becoming more and more wise as time goes by. Each of us is born with particular ingrained and genetically determined traits of our
personality. We have certain strengths which we need to build on.
Some people are naturally logical, some empathic, and some imagi-
native. We should nurture these strengths yet also avoid being
pigeonholed as a specific personality type such as an extrovert or
introvert. Our development depends on expanding our preferences
and using the full spectrum of behaviors available to us. We can be
extrovert or introvert, rational or intuitive, disciplined or spontaneous. We are not just our preferences. We are far more than stereotyped personality. This realization is one of the paths to wisdom.

INTELLIGENCE REVISITED

Because the Take Charge method places high value on such
inner qualities as intuition, creativity, compassion, insight, and
wisdom, people sometimes question our respect for traditional
logic and problem-solving techniques that have sustained companies and organizations throughout our history. Does the Take
Charge process discriminate against plain old cognitive thinking
and everyday rational decision-making?

Definitely not – just the opposite, in fact. What we're doing here is expanding the cognitive decision-making process to include both the power of deductive thought and other invaluable functions of total-brain performance.

As you'll remember, we talked earlier about the five different dimensions of human consciousness and how an integration of these five functions into whole-brain performance is the ultimate aim at all levels of business and organizational action.

Without question, the cognitive deductive power of the logical thinking brain is of vast importance – yet when it is isolated from the other functions, it can become limiting and unreliable.

When Tom learned to use his five-star intelligence, he became a superior decision-maker and improved his chances of becoming a CEO. First, he applied his perceptual function so that he gathered all the available data for making a decision for an acquisition of a competitor; and then he reflected on this data to determine the pros and cons of the acquisition. Then he considered similar past decisions he and his colleagues had made by using his memory effectively.

Tom was already effective at these steps. His breakthrough came when he applied his imagination in a new way to develop a new vision for the planned acquisition. Then he was in optimum position to advance into the more expanded functions of whole-brain intelligence, where he ensured his emotional stance was compassionate and free from debilitating worries and judgments. And finally, he moved to high-level strategic thinking where he was more insightful, creative, and wise.

With the Take Charge method, Tom could see the big picture and engage a far broader range of mental aptitudes for making a decision. Whereas before he might have rejected the acquisition on strictly financial grounds, as the price was too high, now he was able to see the strategic value of the acquisition and also develop creative financing of the deal to ensure that both parties were content.

Following is the powerful "five-star intelligence" process through which our method specifically trains you to move. Please be sure to memorize this problem-solving system, so that whenever you're confronted with a new dilemma, whatever it might be, you can confidently move through the full "five-star intelligence" system to make sure your decision is as rock-solid as possible.

"FIVE-STAR INTELLIGENCE" PROBLEM-SOLVING

1. *USE YOUR* PERCEPTUAL *FUNCTION TO GATHER ALL DATA AVAILABLE.*

2. *EMPLOY YOUR* COGNITIVE-THINKING *FUNCTION TO THE MAX, TO BRAINSTORM RATIONALLY ABOUT YOUR DILEMMA.*

3. *ADD YOUR* MEMORY/IMAGINATION *FUNCTION TO PROVIDE DEPTH OF PERSPECTIVE AND A BEGINNING SENSE OF THE FUTURE PLAN.*

4. *ACTIVATE YOUR* DEEPER EMOTIONAL *FUNCTION, SO THAT YOU PUT ASIDE ANXIETY AND NEGATIVE EMOTIONAL REACTIONS AND TAP THE POWER OF COMPASSION AND EMOTIONAL INTELLIGENCE.*

5. *SHIFT INTO YOUR* FIFTH-INTELLIGENCE *FUNCTION WHERE YOU EXPAND YOUR EXPERIENCE TO INCLUDE THE INTUITIVE "SEEING THE WHOLE AT ONCE," OPEN TO FLASHES OF INTEGRATED INSIGHT, AND TURN TO YOUR CORE OF WISDOM FOR THE FINAL EXPANSION INTO FIVE-STAR INTELLIGENCE.*

Probably, you already habitually move through the first three problem-solving steps. The Take Charge method makes sure that you break beyond the strictures of deductive thought and add the final two primary functions of the mind in the equation.

A wise decision is more than high-powered thinking.
A wise decision is one that the whole brain and body
in total expanded consciousness "know" is right.
That whole-body sense of connection is from where
your power to act with certainty emerges.

Wise leaders radiate that sense of "feeling connected" with the depths of their own intelligence and wisdom. This sixth step of the Take Charge process does exactly that: aims your full attention toward feeling connected. You will be able to integrate your different modes of thinking and feeling, and make better decisions.

You do have a wise inner center to your being – but if
you don't regularly aim your attention there, you
remain, for all intents and purposes, disconnected from
your center. And who wants to follow a leader who
doesn't feel connected with his or her inner center of
intelligence, compassion, and wisdom?

TAKE CHARGE UPLIFT 6: WISE LEADERSHIP

Your career will depend at many levels on your readiness to assume responsibility for making wise decisions, so set aside at least three times a day (just a few minutes each time) to move through this process until you make it your own. Memorize the words or listen to the online audio guidance until you truly know this process by heart.

To approach your inner source of wisdom and empowerment, take time to pause, become quiet . . . and experience the special evocative power of these focus words . . .

Now, exhale, hold on empty, and say, "I give myself permission to feel good." Allow your next inhale to rush in through your nose . . . and a general sense of feeling good to fill your heart and body . . .

Then say, in turn:

"I let go of my worries and feel peaceful in my mind."

"I let go of judging and accept reality just as it is."

"I accept and love myself, just as I am."

"I'm open to receive insight and inspiration."

And now, when you're ready, say the sixth Focus Phrase and allow your mind's full attention to look inward and experience the actual feeling of being connected with your source of insight and wisdom. Say: "I feel connected with my inner source of wisdom."

Each time you say these words, let yourself look deeper, feel more connected, open up to new insights and vision . . .

PAUSE & EXPERIENCE

CHAPTER 8

ACT WITH INTEGRITY

CHAPTER 8: PREVIEW

Core Need – Act with Integrity: Recent research shows an increasing need for employees to find purpose and significance at work. Employees want to work for an ethical organization and feel that they're working with integrity. Similarly, employers want their staff to feel profound commitment to the mission of the organization. Research has also shown that businesses that are serious about social responsibility are also more profitable.

Our Solution: Our process leads you into a profound change of mind, in which you discover that you have an inner core that is honest, wise, and dedicated. By regularly making contact with your own source of integrity, you optimize your power to act with courage and vision.

The Process: To awaken your own sense of certainty and dedication, you must first state your intent – and then go into action to manifest your intent. This step of the Take Charge method shifts you into demonstrating rightful action at work.

Your Payoff: Acting with integrity and certainty is a powerful source of motivation – so that you act with courage and conviction and value your at-work life as an arena where you can advance your personal development and ethics while you also earn your living.

DILEMMA AT WORK

Philip got his big break when he took over the regional office of his company in Chicago last year. He started his reign as head of the region by pushing his employees even harder than his predecessor. He demanded longer hours and insisted that total devotion to the company's bottom line be the required sacrifice, even if it meant undercutting family time and enjoyment at work. This was how his old boss had pushed him, so he assumed it would also work now that he was in charge. His primary motivation was to engender such good work in his Chicago division that he'd get promoted again, this time to the New York head office.

Driven by his own selfish goals, Philip fired several long-term employees of the company who resisted his reign, and put fear in the hearts of everyone else. People stayed later at the office and worked harder. The stress level was a clear indicator that employees were pushing to their limits. But after the first quarter of his Chicago reign the financial results were not good – increased pressure and stress on the job had not increased productivity and sales. Plus employee morale was way down; the brightness of positive attitude that he'd inherited at the office had diminished, and creativity was way down. No one dared speak up against his ideas, and some of his ideas had not worked at all. Plus there was a noted rise in colds and flu sick-leaves. Worst of all, Philip felt that he wasn't really respected, let alone liked, as the leader of the team. He felt alienated and unable to rally his team to deliver results.

Philip was a masterful executive and there was no reason for him not to rise to the top – except that he wasn't wise about the true qualities of leadership. As we'll see in this chapter, the only thing that could save him from losing his position of leadership would be an inner willingness to change his attitudes about leadership. He also needed to wake up to the fact that true leadership is servant leadership, not selfish leadership. This seventh step of our Take Charge method provides the impetus and process for becoming a wiser, more respected and effective leader at all levels of participation.

Everyone wants to follow leaders who are intelligent, honest, creative, compassionate, and wise. The first six steps of the Take Charge program aim to help you develop such inner qualities. Now, in this final, seventh step, it's time for you to take what you've gained from moving through the process and turn your attention again outward to the world as you move into action gear.

By the time you arrive at this final Focus Phrase, you have put aside most of the fear-based and ego-based intentions that tend to limit your vision and personal power. You've expanded your awareness to include empathy in your heart, the clarity of non-judgment in your mind, plus a solid sense of intuitive insight and connectedness with your core wisdom and intelligence. And in so doing, you've aimed your personal intent beyond purely selfish machinations, toward working for the benefit of your colleagues, your organization, and your customers.

This seventh Focus Phrase clarifies (loud and clear)
that you intend, with your coming action,
to help yourself prosper and enjoy life and,
at the same time, to be of service to others.
The words of this final statement of intent are quite clear:
"I am here to serve, to prosper, and to enjoy myself."

These words fully support your personal needs and also the
needs of your teammates, customers, family, and community. This
is the philosophy of "servant leadership," where one of your primary roles as an employee or leader is to support others in getting
what they want and need. After all, every job or position in a company or organization involves serving others – your colleagues,
your customers, your shareholders, and your community.

The concept of service turns the conventional
organizational hierarchy upside down.
You shift your focus from control and
command to support and encouragement.

You will find that the first six Focus Phrases naturally lead you
into this expanded, compassionate, empowered state of mind in
which service to others is as important as serving yourself. All
organizations, by definition, are built on this assumption of mutu-
ality and service. Now we are suggesting that you openly state this

intent to yourself, so that you clearly and cleanly align yourself with your deeper purpose as you move into renewed action at work.

As you say these words, "I am here to serve, to prosper, and to enjoy myself," over and over for a week or two, you'll find that the words carry great impact. They empower you in a way that purely selfish intent simply cannot.

As purely selfish assumptions about leadership start to crumble and be replaced by the powerful principle of mutual service, you'll find that all aspects of your performance at work become enhanced. Why is this? Because when you purposefully serve others and integrate your personal intent with the greater intent of your organization, you gain more authentic power than when you are simply serving yourself.

A solid example of this is the case of Philip, the fast-rising executive we met at the beginning of this chapter. When he moved to Chicago to take over that division of his company, he went into super-high gear to push his employees even faster than they'd been working before. This of course made him stressful as well, and his wife insisted that he get a physical checkup. He found a good doctor who expressed concern about Philip's blood pressure, which was high even with medication. As an effective non-drug remedy the doctor suggested that Philip learn the Take Charge method and prescribed practicing the three-minute version of the method on an hourly basis at work, to help Philip lower his blood pressure and reduce his general stress condition. Philip was afraid of having a stroke, as his father had, so he diligently studied and mastered the Take Charge process, then just like he regularly did his physical exercises to stay in shape and healthy, he developed a daily routine doing the Full-Mind Workout.

One of the valuable side effects of regularly practicing the Take Charge process at work was that when Philip came to the sixth and seventh steps of the method, he began to realize, through pausing to see the larger picture at work, that he wasn't really serving his employees at all. He was actually abusing them in order to push his own career and self-image so he could have a shot at running the New York office.

When Philip paused and expanded his awareness to "perceive the whole" of his regional office, he could see that his employees were being pushed heartlessly beyond their limits. And as he explored the new idea (for him) of acting with integrity at work, he more and more chafed at his attitudes and decisions that were pushing his employees into stress and no-fun states of mind at work. Furthermore, he knew that most of his employees had families they were having to neglect in favor of supposed loyalty to the company.

After several weeks, Philip made a decision: to do what he knew in his heart was right and to stand firm with his own superiors if they reacted to his new executive approach. He first of all gave all his employees five minutes free each hour, so they could shift into more enjoyable states at work and regain their inner sense of composure and balance. He then called a meeting and informed everyone that he was reversing his policy. No longer

INTEGRITY

would he demand extra hours on the job when he knew his employees also had responsibilities at home.

He granted them breathing space in their lives to live full lives – and, in the same breath, he gave them the challenge of using the new freedom to explore new ways to make their company succeed. He also provided all the cognitive training and tools they needed to make a major positive shift in company atmosphere and performance.

The results were remarkable – suddenly, the atmosphere in all five regional offices relaxed, became more friendly and enjoyable. Unexpected insights and breakthroughs opened up new markets and expanded existing ones. His employees actually enjoyed arriving at work, absenteeism dropped significantly, and the general physical health of employees rose considerably. By actively serving his employees, Philip discovered he served his company and himself as well. He now loved getting to work, being greeted by smiling faces and winning minds. Furthermore, his own family suddenly gained a new sense of togetherness and integrity.

KNOWING WHAT'S RIGHT

On a smaller scale, Philip found that he could now approach challenging decisions in a new way. Decision-making is of course a primary activity at work. And as we've seen, the best decisions emerge not from the purely deductive conclusions of one function of the mind, but from an integrated action of the entire mind, in which the "everything at once" creative and intuitive power of the mind is combined with the power of deduction.

A primary quality of a true and trusted leader at any level of an organization is this person's inner sense of "knowing" what is right to do in a situation – and then acting confidently on it, with a clear sense that the decision is positive and correct. Such leadership, as Philip discovered, also inspires others with confidence and gives them a clear sense of direction. A feeling of greater certainty and confidence, as well as group strength, emerged in his company as everyone discovered their latent leadership powers and capacity for acting with inner harmony.

Throughout this book, you've been exploring how you can encourage this total-mind sense of integration, clarity, wisdom, and perspective. Now you're ready to put this inner certainty into action yourself – as you evaluate a new situation, gain an overview of the whole, tap your total-mind intuition and connection with your underlying source of wisdom – and then move into action.

You probably know from experience what we mean when we talk about that inner feeling of certainty that can come to you when you know your decision is right. This inner certainty is partly generated by employing data and deduction, but it also comes from the deeper integrative function of the mind. And yes, it's more than a thought; it's a whole-body feeling of certainty.

During the 1980s and 1990s, there was a concerted move-

INTEGRITY

ment in business circles to bad-mouth this inner feeling of certainty. We were supposed to put aside all our "soft intuitive" hunches and instead trust nothing but hard data and logical deduction. This was despite the widespread recognition that, in most innovative business decisions, there is never enough hard data to generate one-hundred percent certainty in the decision-making process.

Far too many executives bought into the psychologically invalid attitude that the four dimensions of human consciousness, beyond the deductive, were neither valuable nor dependable in making decisions. These more subtle mental qualities were held suspect because computers couldn't locate them on their two-dimensional screens and, furthermore, too many hot-shot executives had themselves lost touch with these higher functions of the mind.

Philip had lost touch with his inner certainty and for years had pushed with selfish decisions and narrow-minded logic. His high blood pressure was partly caused by an underlying chronic anxiety, arising from his lack of that deeper sense of knowing what is right to do.

When he rediscovered his power to tap a higher level of certainty in his decisions, his blood pressure stopped spiking and his stress dropped. He acted with confidence and a good feeling in his whole body that he was working for the higher good and being of valuable service not only to his family and company, but to his greater community as well.

Let's stop a moment or two here, so that you have time to reflect on your own present feelings and opinions regarding all this.

Tune in to your breathing . . . your heart . . . your body in this present moment . . . and listen to your emerging thoughts about your personal ability to look to the heart of a difficult decision . . . and through truly seeing the situation clearly, know what is right to do.

Do you indeed possess all five dimensions of consciousness – and are you willing to trust all five dimensions at once to generate your next decision and move you into confident action to manifest that decision?

PAUSE & REFLECT

CHARISMA ON DEMAND

One of the main benefits of regularly moving through the Take Charge process is that you steadily develop wisdom and effective decision-making. An equally important benefit is that you are, at the same time, nurturing charisma in its true expression.

Here's the generic dictionary definition of "charisma":
 . . . from the original Greek *kharisma* (divine

gift) and *kharis* (favor) (1) a personal quality attributed to those leaders who arouse fervent popular devotion and enthusiasm; (2) personal magnetism or charm; (3) *(in Christianity)* an extraordinary power granted by the Holy Spirit.

In our nonreligious context here, we're focusing on the first two definitions.

Curiously, if you take a look once again (see below) at the seven primary qualities we identified as vital to wisdom, you'll notice that these qualities apply equally to a person with charisma.

THE CHARISMATIC PERSON

- A person who radiates a powerful sense of whole-body groundedness in the present moment

- A person who's confident and brave emotionally, free from anxieties and apprehensions about the future

- A person with a quiet, receptive mind that is not judgmental or prejudiced

- A person who is full of compassion and self-acceptance, and radiates empathy

- A person who is often intuitively inspired and can see the whole situation

- A person who regularly tunes in to his or her deeper inner source of wisdom and "knowing"
- A person who is confident, dynamic, and magnetic, and ready to take action and serve others

If you want to be someone who is respected, regularly exudes charisma, and inspires coworkers into positive action – if you want to rise to the top as a leader, then you must devote regular time to nurturing the seven qualities just outlined.

Furthermore, when you need to tap some "charisma on demand," you will want to move quickly through the full Take Charge process, in one to three minutes – and charge your whole being with those exact qualities that will give you charisma.

BECOME THE LEADER

Each workday presents you with multiple opportunities, large and small, to activate your charisma and lead with wisdom and power. Probably, if you're like most people, in most situations you're currently not fully rising to the fore and offering your leadership potential.

Let's ask a few questions for you to reflect on to clarify certain aspects of this process.

INTEGRITY

As preparation for reflecting on the following questions (or on any topic), you will always benefit by first moving through the four Wake Up steps you learned in chapter 1.

Tune in to the air flowing in and out of your nose . . . expand your awareness to include the movements in your chest and belly as you breathe . . . expand to also be aware of the feelings in your heart . . . and expand to be aware of your whole body, here in this present moment . . .

Now, in this quiet, expanded state of mind, read each of the following questions one at a time as you stay aware of your breathing . . . and after each question, as you continue to stay aware of your breathing and the feelings in your heart, see what thoughts and insights come spontaneously as you reflect on the questions:

Are you wanting to generate more wisdom and leadership power in your life, or are you content with your present levels of wisdom and power?

If being a wise leader means putting aside personal ego games in order to evaluate and act on a situation from an expanded view of the whole – are you ready to assume this dispassionate stance?

If wise action requires letting go of selfish habits and nonstop material accumulation, so that you act on a dedication to the higher good beyond personal success, are you ready to do this?

If true leadership means putting long-term and sustainable results ahead of short-term gain, are you ready to take this leap? Do you agree that leadership requires a dimension of serving others – or do you prefer to run your life focused only on serving yourself?

Do you feel that you can serve others and, at the same time, fully serve and enjoy yourself?

When you go into action at work after making a decision, where does your underlying sense of rightness and certainty in your action come from?

PAUSE & REFLECT

WISDOM IN ACTION

If you found that you resonated with these questions, and if you're willing to practice the method we're teaching here, then you will most definitely be able to nurture your seven leadership qualities, become a consistently trustworthy person in your business life, and enjoy the benefits thereof – not because you're someone unusually blessed or special, but because you're someone who has taken on the responsibility of managing your mind to aim toward your chosen intent.

How does this translate into your everyday work environment? How do you apply what you're learning into a concrete game plan? Here's an action game plan based on the five-star process of the last chapter.

FIVE-STAR WISDOM PROCESS

1. *WITH EACH NEW DECISION OR DILEMMA YOU APPROACH, FIRST MOVE THROUGH THE WAKE UP PROCESS (THE FOUR-STEP METHOD YOU LEARNED IN CHAPTER 1) TO MAKE SURE YOU'RE ALERT AND BRIGHT.*

2. *NOW SPEND HOWEVER MUCH TIME YOU NEED IN YOUR USUAL DEDUCTIVE MODE OF INFORMATION COLLECTION, REFLECTION, AND ACTIVE LOGICAL PROBLEM-SOLVING.*

3. *NOW PAUSE, AND CHOOSE TO SHIFT INTO A MORE EXPANSIVE "ALL AT ONCE" PERSPECTIVE. MOVE THROUGH THE FIRST FIVE STEPS OF THE FULL TAKE CHARGE PROCESS, AND OPEN UP TO WHATEVER INSIGHTS COME TO YOU.*

4. *NOW, WITH AN EXPANDED MIND AND HEART FULLY ENGAGED, SAY THE SIXTH FOCUS PHRASE, "I FEEL CONNECTED WITH MY SOURCE OF WISDOM," AND FOR JUST A FEW MOMENTS, WITH YOUR*

THINKING MIND QUIET, BREATHE INTO THAT BASIC SENSE OF CONNECTION WITH YOUR SOURCE OF PERSONAL GUIDANCE AND REALIZATION.

5. NOW REFLECT AGAIN FROM THIS DEEPER PERSPECTIVE ON THE DECISION YOU FACE, AND ASK YOURSELF, "WHAT'S THE WISE THING TO DO HERE?"

6. NOW SIMPLY BREATHE, STAY QUIET IN YOUR MIND, AND ALLOW YOUR DEEPER INTELLIGENCE TO RISE UP AND SPEAK IN WHATEVER WAY IT CHOOSES.

7. TUNE IN TO AND ACCEPT YOUR INSPIRED THOUGHTS AND FEELINGS OF WHAT TO DO IN THIS NEW SITUATION, AND THEN, WITH AN INNER SENSE OF CERTAINTY, SAY TO YOURSELF THE SEVENTH FOCUS PHRASE, "I AM HERE TO SERVE, TO PROSPER, AND TO ENJOY MYSELF." IN THIS SPIRIT AND WITH THIS PRIMARY INTENT, GO INTO ACTION TO MANIFEST YOUR DECISION.

INTEGRITY

BUILT TO BE USED

Every time you move through this process, you'll get better and better at it. Think of when you learned to walk, to ride a bicycle, to drive a car. At first, you have to move step-by-step and even struggle to accomplish the process. But soon you develop a new habit so that you perform the process fast, confidently, and successfully.

So just move enjoyably through the "wise decision and action" process for a few weeks without expecting great flashes. Get good at the process; then when the process becomes habitual and empowered, you will be able to tap the deeper resources of the technique for the rest of your life.

You'll also find that you can write and deliver excellent speeches in this state of mind. You can negotiate with power and fairness, make family and relationship decisions at home that resonate with certainty and truth, and, in general, run your life through the guidance of your inherent sense of wise action.

You now have in hand the basic tools to advance your life. But having a shovel, hoe, and seeds in the garage does not get your garden planted or your crop harvested. The key element is always your own intent and where you choose to focus your power of attention.

BEYOND GREED AND SELFISHNESS

Several mental habits and ingrained attitudes can directly short-circuit the emergence of your inherent wisdom and leadership power. Let's bring these to the fore. Once you see them clearly, you can begin to let go of them consciously and advance into attitudes that serve you better.

For instance, people like Philip was before his shift into integrity – selfishly attached to the outcome of a situation and wanting to grab as much as they can for themselves – won't be able to make a genuinely wise decision because, by definition, they're not wanting to see what's best for everyone involved and what's optimum for the situation.

People who are just out for number one and screw everybody else are not in a position to serve the higher good and represent a group or organization. Selfishness and wisdom do not live in the same heart.

Each moment choose to base your decisions and actions on your wisdom, not on fear and selfishness.

Philip had the habit of waking up around five in the morning and immediately jamming his mind to come up with new angles for his success at work. When he started monitoring his blood pressure, he found that the base numbers jumped up dangerously during this mental-jam period of the day.

Talking with his new doctor, he saw the greater whole of his behavior: He was regularly using his mind in a way that was damaging his body. If he continued doing this (on the assumption that it made him succeed at work), in the long run he'd perhaps have a stroke or heart attack and make his family suffer.

Seeing and accepting the greater picture, Phil did the right thing. He made the inner decision not to spend early mornings in tense brainstorming. Instead, he developed the positive habit of doing the Spiral Process (see chapter 10) each morning, and then doing some physical exercising. The results pleased him. Not only did his blood pressure stop spiking during those hours, he also found that, in the middle of a quiet contemplative mind, ideas began popping up effortlessly and with no stress at all, which propelled him into a higher level of success than he ever imagined.

Philip changed his deeper qualities of heart and mind – he shifted from being selfish to being of service to his family, his company, and his community. As a result, his superiors began seeing him in a new, greater leadership role. As he became grounded in service to others, he actually served himself as well.

Please note that we're not in any way saying that you shouldn't look out for number one in life. We all have our right to strive for a good life and enjoy ample material benefits. That's why the seventh Focus Phrase is stated just as it is: "I am here to serve, to prosper – and to enjoy myself." This wording integrates all three of our primary human needs.

But selfishness and greed are quite different from a healthy desire to live the good life – because both selfishness and greed are ultimately based on fear rather than on love. When you're compassionate, you want to take your fair share and make sure that the people around you get their fair share.

Philip discovered that when he made his employees' lives as important as his own, their team effort surged and everyone benefited. A team acting with integrity, serving the organization, attains greater strength and superior results. A team enjoying every new moment is highly creative and effective in communication and sales. This is a great team!

Only when we shift out of our habitual worrying, grabbing, judging, and competing, and focus on compassion, trust, and sharing, can we perceive what is best not only for us, but for our family, our community, and, indeed, for the world – and act to support a sustainable future for us all.

THE STRATEGIC EDGE

As soon as you begin to expand your awareness to include heartfelt interaction with the world around you, you naturally begin to realize that you are not an isolated individual who must fight everyone else to survive. You're connected at a deep level to those around you in your business and community. We're all actually serving each other, every new day, for the common good.

This basic realization, as Philip discovered by using the method, is built into the Take Charge experience. Each time he moved through the seven expansions, he found that he woke up his capacity to see the whole, to act from the heart, and to integrate all aspects of his wisdom into a clear vision of the future of his company.

Strategic planning also, step by step, became second nature to

INTEGRITY

Philip. As he made more contact with his deeper vision of what was best for him, his company, and his community, he found he could tap his true charisma and act with power.

In this light, regularly moving through the Take Charge process can prove key to a more fulfilling life. By repeatedly directing your full attention to make contact with your own integrated presence, you unify all five dimensions of awareness into one unified experience. This is the path of the wise person – which you can freely and enjoyably choose to walk.

THE ENJOYMENT FACTOR

We're almost to the end of our discussion of the Take Charge process, but we've still not talked about the final and essential ingredient in this heady mix. "I am here to serve others, to prosper – and to enjoy myself!" Self-sacrifice might have its place in extremes and every so often in everyday business situations, but, in general, we all have a right not only to serve the higher good, but also to enjoy each moment thoroughly along the way.

Simple psychology dictates the necessity of including pleasure in the equation of wise, powerful leadership. We do gravitate toward pleasure and avoid pain – that's our ingrained nature, so why fight it? We've been given a body that carries remarkable potential for feeling good – and it's both our responsibility and our privilege not to waste this potential.

At work, especially, it's vital to state over and over our intent and our right to enjoy ourselves. Our ongoing challenge is to successfully merge service and pleasure – to discover how to integrate good works and fun times into one seamless experience.

And – the best way to accomplish this is to say it, and then do it! "I am here to serve others and also to enjoy myself!"

Philip actively encouraged feeling good in his company. He made sure that his employees mastered the fine art of letting go of their worries at work, and letting go of damaging judgment as well. He gathered everyone together once a day for a short chat about their experience at work – about the power of feeling good and taking breaks to let the creative muses have a chance to express themselves. His team found that the "enjoy myself" dimension of the intent statement served as the ignition point in truly waking up their greater potential.

So remember to include in your statement of intent, over and over each day at work, the pleasure principle. Yes, you're at work to do your job and get paid and get ahead. But you're also at work to enjoy being alive each and every moment. You spend half your waking life at work. Definitely, it's wise to make sure you enjoy that half of your life!

In the next part of the book, we're going to review everything you've learned in this program, plus teach you some interesting variations on the general theme of taking charge of your mind. To end this chapter, let's just relax and enjoy the power that the seventh Focus Phrase adds to your daily mental-workout routine.

INTEGRITY

TAKE CHARGE UPLIFT 7: INTEGRITY

Take a breather . . . give yourself permission to feel good . . . let go of your worries at work . . . accept people just as they are . . . and also accept yourself just as you are . . . open up to receive intuitive insights and great ideas . . . feel your connection with your inner source of strategic thinking and wisdom . . . and say to yourself several times, "I am here to serve, to prosper – and to enjoy myself!"

As you breathe into these words and their power, be open to a new experience of action imbued with integrity and certainty. . .

PAUSE AND EXPERIENCE

PART FOUR

Strategies/Support

The mind is its own place, and in itself
Can make a heav'n of hell, a hell of heav'n.
- John Milton

C H A P T E R   9

SPECIFIC STRATEGIES AT WORK

DAILY WORKOUT

You have now learned (or are beginning to learn) two special techniques for taking charge of your mind and focusing your power of attention in directions that serve you quite well indeed. You've learned the super-fast one-minute Wake Up process with its four Focus Phrases to bring you immediately to your senses and wake up your charisma. And you're busy mastering the seven-step Take Charge process to expand your awareness fully and activate all five functions of your mind.

Now that you have read through the whole discussion of these twin techniques, it's time to learn them by heart – and then apply them effectively in your at-work environment. So please give yourself time to return to each of the 11 phrases and practice until you master them.

This chapter first gives you a quick review of the full method – for a quick-reference list of all 11 Focus Phrases. Then we offer several detailed strategies regarding how and when to apply these techniques to specific situations at work, and also at home.

Your primary challenge in mastering the overall Take Charge process is, of course, to learn by heart the 11 Focus Phrases – and then regularly move through the process so that you begin to tap the magic they generate. Here in short order is the list of the 11 Focus Phrases. Also go online for further training.

THE WAKE UP PROCESS

This basic one-minute wake up experience can be done on its own or as preparation for the Take Charge program. As a general rule, use the exact words and say the statements as you exhale, so that your mind is quiet to experience the effects of the words on your next inhale.

One: "I feel the air flowing in and out of my nose."
Two: "I also feel the movements in my chest and belly."
Three: "I'm aware of the feelings in my heart."
Four: "I'm aware of my whole body here in this present moment."

You can drop this down even further if you want, once you get good at this – and just say to yourself:

1. Breath . . .
2. Chest and belly . . .
3. Feelings in my heart . . .
4. Whole body at once . . .

The ultimate aim here is to make a sequential process (four sentences, four breaths) an instantaneous process, in which the

DAILY WORKOUT

full expansion instantly happens. This takes practice, but it's in your future.

THE TAKE CHARGE PROGRAM

This two- to three-minute in-depth experience takes you through the full process to tap all five dimensions of awareness, so you operate at maximum performance. As you learned in chapters 2–8, there are variations to some of these wordings to adapt the program to special situations. Please refer to the chapters for details, and be sure to return to the chapters to practice and move deeper into each of the Focus Phrases.

1. "I give myself permission to feel good."
2. "I let go of my worries and feel peaceful inside."
3. "I accept everyone at work, just as they are."
4. "I accept, honor, and love myself, just as I am."
5. "I'm ready to receive insight and inspiration."
6. "I feel connected with my inner source of wisdom."
7. "I am here to serve, to prosper – and to enjoy myself."

These Focus Phrases become more and more powerful each time you say them. With each repetition, you develop a stronger associative response. Soon you'll find that simply by saying one of the Focus Phrases, even on its own, you awaken a great depth of insight and clarity within you, because each of these statements elicits an actual experience, not just a thought.

"FULL-MIND WORKOUT" DAILY FITNESS PROGRAM

This program takes the basic Take Charge method and turns it into a short invigorating daily workout routine, parallel to a physical fitness program. You will perhaps find this the very best way to integrate mental and emotional exercises into your daily schedule. You know how important it is to discipline yourself at least a bit each day to stay in physical shape. It's equally important to develop a discipline for your "full-mind workout" routine.

Each day of your workweek will highlight a different focus phrase and "mental muscle group" workout. This routine will make sure that each new week you exercise and strengthen all five of your mental and emotional areas. Please go online if you want audio guidance through each of these four-minute mental workouts:

Monday: Fitness 1 ~ Strengthen Charisma

During the first minute of this Monday mind/mood workout, you'll move rapidly through the Wake Up process – to exercise your power to expand your awareness all the way to whole-body presence:

One: "I feel the air flowing in and out of my nose."
Two: "I also feel the movements in my chest and belly."
Three: "I'm aware of the feelings in my heart."
Four: "I'm aware of my whole body here in this present moment."

For the second minute (one focus phrase for each new breath) move through the seven-step Take Charge exercise, flexing each of these psychological muscles in turn:

1. "I give myself permission to feel good."
2. "I let go of my worries and feel peaceful inside."
3. "I accept everyone at work, just as they are."
4. "I accept, honor, and love myself, just as I am."
5. "I'm ready to receive insight and inspiration."
6. "I feel connected with my inner source of wisdom."
7. "I am here to serve, to prosper – and to enjoy myself."

Now for the next minute or so, focus intently on Monday's theme and exercise – by saying to yourself three times, "I give myself permission to feel good," with two breaths for each statement. Each time you express this intent, you'll flex this particular "mental/emotional muscle" and develop your power to indeed shift faster and deeper into this "feel good" experience. This is definitely a "muscle" you will want to focus on and strengthen – so that when you really need to shift fast into a brighter mood, you have the power to do so.

For the fourth and final minute of Monday Exercise, you just relax your entire mental and emotional presence, watch your breathing – and allow your basic "expansion power" to flex its ability to become more and more aware in general – so that when you end the Monday Workout you're in optimum mental and emotional condition to plunge back into work.

During the rest of the day, continue to bring to mind Monday's focus phrase, "I give myself permission to feel good," so that you keep strengthening this ability.

Tuesday: Fitness 2 ~ Confidence Boost

Do the Wake Up process in one minute.

Do the Take Charge method in one minute or so.

Say to yourself, "I let go of my worries and feel peaceful in my mind," three times, and go deeply into this exercise and experience.

Say Tuesday's focus phrase often during the day, to boost your sense of confidence and power to act without fear.

Wednesday: Fitness 3 ~ Team Spirit

Do the Wake Up process in one minute.

Do the Take Charge method in one minute or so.

Say to yourself, "I accept everyone on my team, just as they are!" three times, and go deeply into this exercise and experience.

Say Wednesday's focus phrase often during the day, to boost your sense of team spirit and empathy.

Thursday: Fitness 4 ~ Self-Esteem

Do the Wake Up process in one minute.

Do the Take Charge method in one minute or so.

Say to yourself, "I honor and trust and respect myself, just as I am," three times, and go deeply into this exercise and experience.

Say Thursday's focus phrase often during the day, to strengthen your self-esteem.

DAILY WORKOUT

Friday: Fitness 5 ~ Creative Power

Do the Wake Up process in one minute.

Do the Take Charge method in one minute or so.

Say to yourself, "I am open to creative insight," three times, and go deeply into this exercise and experience.

Say Friday's focus phrase often during the day, to exercise your creative powers.

Saturday: Fitness 6 ~ Relax & Reflect

This is a regular day off from exercising your mind – just enjoy yourself!

Sunday: Fitness 7 ~ The Spiral Process

At least for this one day a week, see if you can establish a discipline of setting aside ten to 20 minutes when you move through the full Spiral Process:

Do the Wake Up process;

Move through the Take Charge process once;

Move through the seven steps again;

Move through the process once more . . .

Let your words stop whenever they want to, and experience the deep quality of consciousness you enter into.

Week Two and onward: Repeat the basic pattern of this weekly Full-Mind Workout exercise routine. Each new week, you'll find that you have quite a different experience as you progress through the week – the magnificence of consciousness is that you never have the same experience twice – it's always

DAILY WORKOUT

new. And as you exercise your mind, you'll find that you strengthen "inner mind muscles" that enable you to attain new levels of clarity, creativity, compassion, and charisma. So get in shape – and stay in shape – this is your inner act for attaining more and more personal power and success in life.

Yes, of course, sometimes you'll move through the Take Charge process and not much will happen, especially in the beginning. The human mind is so conditioned to hold on to known fixations that, at first, you'll notice only hints of the depths that await you.

Like all investments, you'll need to put a bit of time and energy in before you begin to receive major rewards. But soon you'll experience enough unexpected bright uplifts that your ego will realize: "Hey, this is definitely worthwhile, this is fun, and it's totally effective."

The ultimate aim of all this mental training is to reach the place where you're able to sustain the expanded Take Charge state of mind almost all the time. That's what true mind management is all about – learning to gain and maintain an expanded state of mind and deeper quality of empathy and creativity at work, so that this heightened level of performance becomes your everyday operational state. It seems that our human nature is to slip back into automatic pilot – so we need to move regularly through the method in order to maintain virtuoso consciousness on the job. This is the game we must play with our minds if we want to keep our mental lights shining brightly.

SPECIFIC APPLICATIONS

You're learning the basic Wake Up/Take Charge method – but exactly how does all this fit into your average workday? There are 14 specific applications we'd like to offer you, crucial moments and situations in which remembering to move through either the Wake Up or the Take Charge process can save your day – and make it much more enjoyable at the same time.

First of all, let's reprint the basic problem-solving technique you learned earlier. You might want to copy and post it in your office or workroom.

SEVEN STEPS FOR GENERATING TRUSTWORTHY DECISIONS

1. WITH EACH NEW DECISION OR DILEMMA YOU APPROACH, FIRST MOVE THROUGH THE WAKE UP PROCESS (THE FOUR-STEP METHOD YOU LEARNED IN CHAPTER 1) TO MAKE SURE YOU'RE ALERT AND BRIGHT.

2. NOW SPEND HOWEVER MUCH TIME YOU NEED IN YOUR USUAL DEDUCTIVE MODE OF INFORMATION

COLLECTION, REFLECTION, AND ACTIVE, LOGICAL PROBLEM-SOLVING.

3. NOW PAUSE, AND CHOOSE TO SHIFT INTO A MORE EXPANSIVE "ALL AT ONCE" PERSPECTIVE. MOVE THROUGH THE FIRST FIVE STEPS OF THE FULL TAKE CHARGE PROCESS, AND OPEN UP TO WHATEVER INSIGHTS MIGHT COME TO YOU.

4. NOW, WITH AN EXPANDED MIND AND HEART FULLY ENGAGED, SAY THE SIXTH FOCUS PHRASE, "I FEEL CONNECTED WITH MY SOURCE OF WISDOM," AND FOR JUST A FEW MOMENTS, WITH YOUR THINKING MIND QUIET, BREATHE INTO THAT BASIC SENSE OF CONNECTION WITH YOUR SOURCE OF PERSONAL GUIDANCE AND REALIZATION.

5. AND NOW, REFLECT AGAIN FROM THIS DEEPER PER- SPECTIVE ON THE DECISION YOU FACE, AND ASK YOURSELF: "WHAT'S THE WISE THING TO DO HERE?"

6. NOW SIMPLY BREATHE, STAY QUIET IN YOUR MIND, AND ALLOW YOUR DEEPER INTELLIGENCE TO RISE UP AND SPEAK IN WHATEVER WAY IT CHOOSES.

DAILY WORKOUT

7. *TUNE IN TO AND ACCEPT YOUR THOUGHTS AND FEELINGS OF WHAT TO DO IN THIS NEW SITUATION — AND THEN, WITH AN INNER SENSE OF CERTAINTY, SAY TO YOURSELF THE SEVENTH FOCUS PHRASE, "I AM HERE TO SERVE, TO PROSPER, AND TO ENJOY MYSELF." IN THIS SPIRIT AND WITH THIS PRIMARY INTENT, GO INTO ACTION TO MANIFEST YOUR DECISION.*

FOURTEEN TAKE CHARGE OPPORTUNITIES

Here's a list of 14 typical situations where you might tend to lose your heads-up awareness, or would value a quick uplift or insight boost to help you stay alert, empathetic, creative, insightful, and wise.

First Thing in the Morning

How you feel when you wake up in the morning will set the tone for the whole day. Remember to observe your mental condition even before you get up. And as a very good habit, even before you get out of bed, move through the four-step Wake Up process, and also the Take Charge experience if you have time, so that you start the day at your best.

In Transit

Most of us get caught hurrying to work – and in the process increase our level of stress. Watch this tendency, and when you find yourself anxiously hurrying, immediately take out your mental first-aid kit of Focus Phrases (either the basic four-step Wake Up process or the seven-step Take Charge experience) and regain your senses and peace of mind. In fact, while commuting is always an excellent time to practice your Focus Phrases, explore new insights, do a solid mental workout – and in general nurture your sense of personal power and well-being.

At the Computer

What a challenge it can be, to remain aware of your breathing and stay calm and centered while pounding away at the computer. But it's worth the training and practice to tune in regularly to your full presence while working at the computer. Here's the essential payoff: You'll become more creative at the computer, you'll write with more depth and power, and you'll enjoy each moment if you stay aware of that air flowing in and out of your nose.

In Meetings

Face-to-face encounters in meetings tend to collapse your awareness, tense your emotions, shut down your empathy, and impinge on your creativity. Therefore, it's vital to manage your mind carefully and continually in meetings. No one will know if you regularly say to yourself, "I feel the air flowing in and out of my nose," or perhaps, "I accept everybody here, just as they are," or "I am open to insight into this dilemma we're trying to solve." All people will notice is that you shine brightly more predictably than most others.

DAILY WORKOUT

With Customers

Customer experience is all-important. And everything we've said is vital when it comes to dealing successfully with customers. Sales is an especially challenging role at work because there are so many pressures and you're "on" so much of the time – with little time to relax and regain your center. Again, no one is stopping you from holding your primary focus on your breathing, your heart, your whole body here in the present moment. Furthermore, sales is all about accepting the customer, being empathetic, and loving yourself so that you radiate good feelings, which, in turn, encourage sales and success. So taking a couple of minutes once an hour to move through the Take Charge process can boost your charisma and sales considerably.

While Brainstorming

It's so easy to get caught in anxious tensions and abstract rumination when you're struggling with a problem you need to resolve. The mind gets tired of being pushed and pressured into coming up with a creative answer to a dilemma. At a certain point, you need to just stop all the exhausting thoughts, take a few minutes to move through the full Take Charge process, and, as you come to the fifth and sixth steps of the process, take a bit of time to tap your deeper resources of creativity, insight, and wisdom.

Coffee Break

Most offices offer artificial stimulants to provoke your brain and body into further work. Whether or not you go for the coffee, please remember that a work break is a vital opportunity to run through either the Wake Up or the full Take Charge process, so that you can quickly rejuvenate your energy system, shift into pleasure mode, and wake up to your deeper presence and charisma at work. If you're lucky, your employer will begin giving you Take Charge breaks on a regular, even hourly basis. It makes good business sense, so don't be surprised if your company begins encouraging you to pause and refresh regularly.

When Conflicts Arise

Being at work almost always involves occasional misunderstandings and conflicts between you and your colleagues or customers. Conflict resolution and the Take Charge process go hand in hand. If in the heat of a conflict you can remember to pull back enough to make contact with your breathing, with your heart, with your whole-body presence, and yes, give yourself permission to feel good right then – you can be the one who initiates better feelings, sees a heartfelt resolution to the conflict, and makes the step toward empathy and mutual satisfaction in the conflict. For more guidance in conflict resolution, check out our website support system (http://takechargetraining.com).

Fighting Fatigue

We all get tired at work, especially if we operate mostly on automatic, lose our awareness of our bodies, and fail to maintain a feeling of pleasure that stimulates alertness and action. As soon as you turn to your breathing, it will deepen. As soon as you turn attention to your heart, you'll wake up to the inflow of good feelings. As soon as you give yourself permission to feel good, you'll brighten and expand your consciousness into more engagement with the situation at work. The Wake Up process is always available to perform that quick pick-me-up.

When Anxiety Grips You

As we've seen, a worried mind is always a detriment to good work and a good life. Be alert to when your mind gets caught up in anxieties large or small, and move through the Take Charge program to break free from the grip of worried thoughts that lead to anxious feelings and drops in performance.

Relaxing after Work

So often, we get off work but carry the tensions and buzz of the workday home with us. Many people turn on the TV or grab a beer or other intoxicant and just zone out after work. Yes, this sometimes does the trick. But also hold in mind that while commuting home or in your home environs, you can put the Take Charge process to work – and quickly shift into more enjoyable, relaxed, rewarding states of mind and body. Start with "I give myself permission to feel good," and then encourage peace of mind . . . let go of judgments you're carrying from work, be your own best friend . . . and manage your mind so that life is bright and your heart singing after work.

Mealtime

Whether it's breakfast on the run, a quick lunch at work, or a hurried dinner – when we eat on automatic, we tend to gobble, not enjoy the food much, and, with our chronic tensions, not digest the food well either. Experiment just before eating by making a short blessing-pause during which you simply move through the four steps of the Wake Up process – and shift into sensory awareness, a state in which the pleasures of eating are truly enjoyed.

Reflection Time

We highly recommend that once a day you find time to pause for ten to 15 minutes and go deeply into the magic of the expanded Take Charge experience that we're going to teach you in the next chapter – the Spiral Process. The Take Charge method expands naturally into a full-blown longer meditation-reflection practice that can truly transform your life.

A Good Night's Sleep

A great many people find that they can't turn their minds off and relax into the embrace of much-needed sleep. We recommend moving through all 11 Focus Phrases when you're lying in bed and can't drift off into dreamland. Say the four Wake Up statements to quiet your mind and regain the present moment, and then, starting with "I give myself permission to feel good," move through the seven Take Charge experiences. Go another round after that if you need to. Almost surely, by the time you start to say the Focus Phrases a third or fourth time, you'll be drifting off . . . feeling good in your body . . . at peace in your heart.

DAILY WORKOUT

Each of these 14 opportunities for a Take Charge Uplift can prove of great value. Your challenge will be to remember to go into positive action every time you are in one of these 14 situations!

Please take advantage of the various additional suggestions and guided programs for the strategies just detailed offered at http://takechargetraining.com. You can even bookmark the main programs you want to remember on your desktop, so that in just a flash you have visual and audio reminders and guided programs to help.

ONE-LINER POWER

Thus far we've mostly emphasized the power of the Take Charge Focus Phrases when said together and in proper order. Indeed, there is great power in that sequential approach to the Focus Phrases. There's another great way you can use these particular statements, however, to deepen and enliven your workday.

We call this alternate game plan the "random-play" approach to consciousness management – where you allow just one of the Focus Phrases to rise spontaneously to the surface of your mind and, rather than just saying it once, hold this sentence in your mind as a quiet, repeating background thought to all you're doing.

As mentioned before, it's all too common for the mind to fixate chronically on particular thoughts, memories, imaginations, worries, or other upsetting or limiting ideas. When the mind runs on automatic, the recurrent thoughts can be mostly subliminal, but they still have their effect. Likewise, you probably know the experience of not being able to get a dumb tune out of your mind, hour after hour.

If you find that recurrent thoughts are dragging you down, or if you want to do something to boost your life, we suggest that you consciously replace such neutral or bothersome one-liners with words that, in and of themselves, will help point your attention in useful and enjoyable directions.

All you need to do is remember the seven
Focus Phrases of the Take Charge process,
and choose the best one for each situation.

Often the sentence that pops first to mind will be the one that will be most beneficial to hold in mind as you go through your day. So go ahead and allow this sentence to run through your mind, play with it, experiment with different tones of voice in which to say it to yourself – have fun with it while you also allow the power of the words to touch you deeply.

You can allow the words to become very quiet, almost subliminal, and they will still offer a steady focus in a direction that you value.

CHOOSE YOUR THEME

As another option, when you face a particular situation, you can also choose the Focus Phrase that will best support you in that situation. The following brief discussions of each Focus Phrase in turn explore how and when you can benefit most from holding a positive Take Charge one-liner in mind as you go about your day.

"I give myself permission to feel good."

This is obviously the most direct statement to hold in mind when you want immediate relief and better feelings to spring into being and brighten your day. The special value of saying this statement is that it moves you naturally through the Wake Up process and also expands your awareness of the world around you through all your senses. A great many people have negative one-liners that make them feel bad. This is the override statement that you can let fill your mind as a backdrop for everything else you're doing, to guarantee that you're getting the most out of life, each and every moment.

"I let go of my worries and feel peaceful inside."

How often do you find yourself caught in worries of one kind or another? If you're like most people, the answer is all too often. If worrying is a habit, then make a habit of holding in your mind these words, so that you directly override your habits and develop an ever-expanding worry-free zone in your mind.

"I accept everyone, just as they are."

As soon as you find yourself caught up in negative or hostile thoughts about a person, group, company, or whatever, just begin to say this one-liner to yourself – and allow the words to ease you out of your judgmental state of mind, into one of acceptance. The relief is fast and the impact on your relating and communicating of great value.

"I accept myself, just as I am."

Again – most of us don't. Instead, we spend too much of each day thinking negative thoughts about ourselves and fixating on old attitudes that undermine our sense of self-worth and esteem. Does this habit make you feel good? If not, just make the slight effort (it will actually be a pleasure) to hold this statement in your mind as you go about your daily routines. Regardless of your mood, you'll find that the words can elicit a momentary feeling of loving yourself just as you are – and this feeling will transform everything you do. Self-love is the ultimate power because it liberates your spirit to shine. So be your own best friend – not because you have to, but because you want to.

"I am open to receive."

DAILY WORKOUT

This, of course, is the primary thought to hold in your mind when you're wanting to make a breakthrough in a problem or challenge, or when you're uncertain about what to do with your life. By shortening the sentence as we have here, the words carry a universal power to open your heart and mind to receive whatever it is you need at that moment.

"I feel connected with my source of wisdom."

Here we have eight words that turn your attention directly toward the source of your creativity, your inspiration, your next breath, and, indeed, your life itself. What a wonderful feeling it is to hold this thought in your mind and allow the words to encourage this feeling of being connected with rather than disconnected from the inner animating power of life. Whenever you want the ultimate uplift, say these words that connect you with the power and love that sustain you at your core.

"I am here to serve, prosper . . . and enjoy myself!"

When you hold this complete statement of active intent running through your mind as background music, the words will work wonders in helping you stay bright, strong, and, yes, happy.

There you have them – seven sentences that can change your life. You have all the cognitive tools you need. Now it's up to you to get good at and use the tools . . . or just put them away and forget about them. Watch what you do, or don't do, during the next weeks. Observe if you have an underlying habit of remaining in "perpetual seeker" gear, rather than shifting into "I finally found it" gear. So many people jump from one thing to another, seeking an ultimate trick or quick-fix method that will somehow relieve them of all the negative pressures that otherwise consume their lives. Staying stuck in this "seeker" gear is both frustrating and fruitless.

We encourage you to break beyond that "seeker" phase and recognize that you now have in hand the tools you were seeking. Now that you've found the proper mental tools, rather than dabbling with them and then putting them aside so you can take off on another hunt, let yourself settle into the more mature phase of life, in which you choose to use the tools that work. This is how you can act to change your life steadily for the better.

> More and more, turn your attention to
> the present moment, where you can be
> most effective and also enjoy life to the fullest.

Right here is where the pleasure lies. This is where the insights appear. This is where you interact with other people and score big at work. This is where it's happening.

So use these Wake Up/Take Charge tools you now have in hand to regularly point your mind's attention where the action is. Discover what your life can feel like when you function with five-star intelligence and whole-brain wisdom. Unleash your true leadership potential – while at the same time setting free your higher creative powers.

Say it – do it!

CHAPTER 10

LONG-TERM TRAINING AND ADVANCEMENT

For most of us, our at-work on-the-job emotional stance is at least somewhat different from our at-home off-work presence. And even though in this program we have been encouraging you to get more in contact with your heart and trust your deeper intuitive insights, we also know that there are required limits on the job in terms of expressing compassion, intimacy, sharing, and trust.

Work can be tough and there are necessary limits to which we all adhere at work, so that we can get a difficult job done and, furthermore, get it done masterfully and on time. The Take Charge techniques are clearly designed to boost your performance and sense of well-being right in the rough-and-tumble atmosphere at work. But this program would not be complete if we ignored the serious challenge of shifting from at-work to at-home mentality and engagement.

> The Take Charge method enables you to shift gears from work to home, and achieve success and happiness in both.

One of the powers of the Take Charge program is that you can use it to integrate who you are at work with who you are at home. In general, the Take Charge program will have a humanizing influence on your life. The very same Take Charge program that you find helpful at work will prove equally helpful at home. At work and at home, you can point your mind's attention in the same valuable, humanizing directions. And you'll reap the same

SPIRAL PROCESS

rewards of being more healthy, more friendly, more responsive in the here and now, more compassionate – and also wiser in your personal decisions and actions.

Here again is the list of where and when you can apply the Take Charge method in your personal life:

Relaxing at Home: So often, we get off work but carry the tensions and buzz of the workday home with us. Even while commuting home or once there, you can do the full Wake Up/Take Charge experience – and quickly shift into a more enjoyable, relaxed, rewarding state of mind and body. Come to your senses, tune in to your heart, get connected with your deeper feelings, and you'll make your friends, mate, and family very happy indeed.

Enjoying Meals: Whether it's breakfast or dinner, you can break the habit of eating on automatic, so that you enjoy not only the food, but also the very breaths you're breathing – and your whole-body experience. Just before eating, you can quietly move through the four steps of the Wake Up process – and shift your focus to the present moment in which the pleasures of eating are truly enjoyed.

Time to Reflect: It is to be hoped that at least once a day you'll find time to pause for ten to 15 minutes as a secular meditation practice and go deeply into the magic of the expanded Take Charge experience that we're going to teach you in a moment – the Spiral Process. The Take Charge method expands naturally into a full-blown, longer meditation-reflection practice.

Sleep Tonight: Too often you might find that you can't turn your worries and relax into much-needed sleep. When you can't drift off into dreamland, we recommend moving through all 11 Focus Phrases. Soon you'll be drifting off . . . feeling good in your body . . . at peace in your heart.

> The Take Charge method will improve
> the quality of your life at work, at home,
> and on holiday. It is always there for you!

Obviously, you can also apply the method whenever else you see fit – there are hundreds of specific applications, which you'll discover in the next weeks. To name just a few, you can use the method when you want to communicate with loved ones more deeply and honestly; when you need to solve a difficult personal problem or family conflict; when you want to break free from a particular worry that's sprung up and grabbed you; or simply when you want to ease up and enjoy the present moment. Go for it!

THE SPIRAL PROCESS

Curiously, the same mental method that can, in one minute, help you become more conscious, empathetic, and creative at work also applies when you want to retreat from the outside world for ten to 20 minutes a day for a deep reflection-meditation experience.

More and more people now maintain at least a ten-minute daily discipline in which they retreat from the world, quiet their minds, and focus their attention inward. This helps them clear their minds, let go of stress, and tune in to their deeper knowledge and values.

We encourage you also to set aside ten to 20 minutes each day, to turn the basic Take Charge process into an instrument for delving deeply into your inner being.
This can make all the difference in your life – and, rather than seeming at odds with your business life, will strengthen the foundation of your business success.

We'll lay out the basic flow of the process for you here. Feel welcome to go online at http://takechargetraining.com for more on this secular approach to meditation – and also for effective audio guidance through the Spiral Process.

The Spiral Process takes the basic linear set of seven Take Charge Focus Phrases that you've learned and transforms them into a spiral that goes round and round . . . for as long as you want to go round and round. You say each of the seven Focus Phrases in proper order, and then, rather than ending the process like you did at work, you return to the first Focus Phrase and move through the seven sentences again – and again – and again.

Here's the vital dynamic to this Spiral Process: Each time you return to the first focus phrase, you'll find that you enter the Spiral at a more sublime level of mental alertness and awareness, and go deeper and deeper as you progress once, twice, three times around the seven-step Spiral. Each new time you say one of the Focus Phrases, you experience the power of this particular focus of attention in a new way.

TOTAL WELLNESS

This Spiral Process is both a physical and emotional wellness program that enables you to quiet your mind, let go of stress, and focus deeply on your expanded presence – with zero religious or esoteric implications. This is a concrete psychological wellness method for relaxing, turning off the worries of the day, and looking quietly inward to your core of being.

The results of this daily reflection-meditation practice can prove far reaching: Old emotional wounds and contractions begin to heal and fade away, negative ingrained attitudes begin to let go, chronic tensions ease up, fears about the future dissipate, and a powerful sense of personal groundedness in one's own true center of being emerges.

SPIRAL PROCESS

So without having to commit to a complex, difficult esoteric meditation ritual, you now have in hand a complete reflection-meditation process to help you be more healthy and also to nurture your deeper sense of connectedness and purpose. This Spiral Process is entirely safe and sound – and fully congruent with the growing research regarding the psychological and medical benefits of reflection and meditation.

And above all, it works. The first time around the Spiral delivers one quality of experience. The second time around delivers an entirely new level of experience. And the third and fourth times around . . . well, begin to practice it yourself, and find out!

Here's a most curious thing that happens when you go round and round on the Take Charge Spiral. At a certain point, as you go round and round, you arrive at a moment in which your ego (who is remembering to say the Focus Phrases) finally falls silent.

You say one of the Focus Phrases – it doesn't matter which one – and rather than your mind remembering to say the next one, instead you move into total quiet in your thinking mind . . . and you emerge into a truly meditative experience that is entirely beyond all words.

This is the deeper reflective aim of the Spiral: to reach that point where all thoughts drop away, even the Focus Phrases, and you enter that expanded state where you are fully integrated, fully aware, and open to embrace an experience that transcends thinking altogether.

More and more research (see the scientific section at the end of this book) demonstrates that entering into this deep state of relaxation on a daily basis enhances well-being, both physically and emotionally. This is the state of consciousness in which you recharge, you heal, and you reestablish your inner sense of integrity and harmony.

> And in this state of expanded mental acuity,
> right in the midst of the quiet and peace,
> sudden insights will often pop into your mind.

This is the great fun of this process, as well as its great value: You never know what is going to rise up as a new insight. You've put yourself in an ideal position for a deep realization or creative flash to come to you. And without any effort or any deliberate intent, you receive what you need.

Sometimes a memory comes to mind and you experience emotional healing. Sometimes you feel intensely your connection with other people or with nature. And sometimes you simply dwell in the calm, peace, and clarity that come to your mind, heart, and soul.

Then at some point, you, of course, begin to move out of your deep state of awareness. The meditative experience has its duration, and then you find more everyday thoughts surfacing and you return to the room around you . . . stretch and open your eyes . . . and either go to bed or reenter your regular routines – feeling much refreshed, perhaps more creative and wiser, and more in touch with your emotions.

SPIRAL PROCESS

OUR FINAL PROGRAM

The Take Charge Spiral

Here is the full Spiral Process. You can do this whenever you have five or more minutes free, even at work. But you'll find it most effective when you have at least ten minutes of free time – perhaps while commuting if you're not driving; perhaps early in the morning before work; or as a relaxation break after work – or at the end of the day before going to bed. You can also do it in bed before going to sleep, when you might drift into sleep.

In whatever way you choose to enter the Spiral, we hope you see it as a lifetime practice that will serve as the daily foundation for maintaining a high level of consciousness, empowerment, and well-being throughout each day!

To begin the Spiral process, find a quiet place where you won't be overly disturbed. Make yourself comfortable either sitting or lying on your back (or perhaps even while walking) . . . close your eyes when you want to . . . and gently remember the four Wake Up Focus Phrases, and say them to yourself one after the other with one or two breaths of silence in between for experiencing.

"I feel the air flowing in and out of my nose."

"I feel the movements in my chest and belly as I breathe."

"I'm aware of the feelings in my heart."

"I'm aware of my whole body, here in this present moment."

When you're ready, you can now move on to the seven Take Charge Focus Phrases . . . say each of the Focus Phrases . . . experience what comes . . . continue moving through the seven steps with two or three breaths of silence between each . . . to the seventh Focus Phrase.

"I give myself permission to feel good."
"I let go of my worries and feel peaceful in my mind."
"I accept everyone I know, just as they are."
"I love myself, just as I am."
"I am open to receive insight and inspiration."
"I feel connected with my source of wisdom."
"I am here to serve, prosper, and enjoy myself!"

After saying the seventh focus phrase, return again to the first Focus Phrase, "I give myself permission to feel good," and say it to yourself again . . . and continue through the seven Focus Phrases again a second time . . . feel free to shorten the phrases a bit if you want to.

When you come to the seventh Focus Phrase, again return to the first Focus Phrase, and move through the process again . . . until your mind finally becomes quiet on its own . . . and you enter into deep reflection and meditation. (Feel free to use our online guidance for this Spiral Process so that you master it effortlessly.)

PAUSE & EXPERIENCE

SPIRAL PROCESS

FINAL WORDS

We've moved a long way quickly in this book, presenting under one cover what would usually take three or four books to accomplish. Congratulations on leaping in and discovering first-hand what the process of consciousness management is all about.

Now comes the most crucial phase – that point where either you put this book down and fail to continue with your training and self-development, or you purposefully choose to continue training, practicing, and advancing with these two powerful mental techniques – until you truly make them your own, merge with them, and live within the expanded consciousness they open up.

As your coaches, we've inspired you as much as we can at this point. We've shown you the whys and the hows of consciousness expansion and full-brain excellence. This book is here so that you can return to the beginning and move through it again, making sure you fully learn the methods. You'll find that the Take Charge method will continue opening up and manifesting new realms of your emerging power and potential. We do hope you'll take the lifelong ride – you deserve it!

ONLINE AUDIO TRAINING AND SUPPORT

http://takechargetraining.com

Often the learning process is facilitated by an audio-training dimension to the program. Therefore we provide a full streamed-audio support system to make sure you learn the Take Charge method by heart. Feel free to enjoy professional yet friendly audio guidance and training for the programs in this book, by going to the website http://takechargetraining.com and taking advantage of all the audio training programs and wellness systems offered there. You'll find an in-depth online course that makes certain you master the Take Charge process, plus daily guidance for the Full-Mind Workout mental fitness program. And of special note – the Take Charge Forum provides an ongoing discussion where you can ask us questions or comment about your experiences. You'll also find a number of other online courses and audio training to further your development and finesse. This site is designed as your long-term support and online Take Charge community. See you there!

DOWNLOADS, CDs, AND DVD TRAINING PROGRAMS

To make sure that you can receive training in all formats, we also offer our various audio guidance and teaching programs in CD and DVD format, so that you can take the audio guidance with you wherever you go. Downloads are also instantly available. Log on at http://takechargetraining.com for further information or to place an order.

WEB HELP

Advanced Business Seminars

Businesses, educational institutions, and government agencies who would like in-house training or custom online training programs, please visit us at http://takechargetraining.com or www.selbysolution.com for further information and scheduling. The authors are also available for public presentations and lectures.

Corporate Application

This book and set of Take Charge mind-management programs can greatly augment a corporation's long-term success through training the entire employee and management team in specific applications to your unique business situation. We offer several pragmatic approaches for full-company training, employing the book, and DVD and online training and support. Feel free to contact us at http://selbysolution.com if you would like consultation on custom applications of this method to your particular corporate needs.

SCIENTIFIC VERIFICATION AND DISCUSSION

Each step in the Take Charge method is the distillation of a set of psychological and organizational skills which are supported by wide-ranging studies. For a more detailed analysis, see Paul Hannam's website at www.phannam.co.uk.

CHAPTER 1: PRESENT-MOMENT EMPOWERMENT

Taking Charge of your mind requires that you are able to shift attention among the past, present, and future dependent on the situation, and this capability has been described as "balanced time perspective" (Boniwell and Zimbardo 2004).

In particular, you need to be able to stay focused in the present moment. This leads to many benefits at work, including improved communication, better time management, higher productivity, and enhanced sense of well-being. By focusing on your breathing and staying in the present moment, you will be practicing a powerful form of meditation throughout the work day. You are training your brain to reap the rewards that one or two daily sessions of intense meditation will bestow, such as improved moods and health.

At the forefront of research in this field is Professor Richard Davidson at the University of Wisconsin, whose brain studies with Buddhist monks were featured in the *Washington Post* in

SCIENCE

January 2005 – "Meditation Gives Brain a Charge, Study Finds." His research provides evidence that meditation can change the workings of the brain, leading to increased levels of awareness and significantly greater activity in the left prefrontal cortex – the area of the brain associated with positive emotions and the goal-seeking behaviors.

This research is following on a long tradition of studies into methods such as Mindfulness, Transcendental Meditation, and the Relaxation response. It is also supported by the concept of "cognitive interference," which examines how attention can be disrupted. Studies by Wickens and Hollands reveal how distractions impact concentration and can lead to impaired performance. Our brains are compared to a computer's working memory, which finds it difficult to cope with overload. In simple terms, if we are ruminating or distracted we take up memory space needed for our task at hand.

When you are sharper, you are able to pay more attention to the tasks at hand, be self-disciplined, and complete the tasks. These are vital skills for success at work and are defined as "conscientiousness" by psychologists. Conscientiousness is one of the "big five" personality factors, a standard model used to measure personality. Moreover, conscientiousness is the most significant factor in predicting job performance (Hurtz and Donovan 2000).

References

Benson, Herbert, and Miriam Z. Klipper. (2001). *The Relaxation Response*. New York: Quill. (First published in 1975.) This very influential book was based on extensive studies at Beth Israel

Hospital and the Harvard Medical School. It proved how relaxation through meditation could promote excellent health, while reducing blood pressure and the risk of heart disease.

Boniwell, I., and P. G. Zimbardo.(2004). "Balancing time perspective in pursuit of optimal functioning." In P.A. Linley and S. Joseph (eds.) *Positive Psychology in Practice.* Hoboken, N.J.: John Wiley & Sons.

Csikszentmihalyi, Mihaly. (1990). *Flow, The Psychology of Optimal Experience.* New York: Harper and Row. The concept of flow refers to the experience of being totally absorbed in present moment activities, and is cited as a core attribute of happy and motivated people.

Hurtz, G. M., and J. J. Donovan. (2000). "Personality and job performance: The Big Five revisited." *Journal of Applied Psychology,* 85, 869–879.

Kabat-Zinn, John. (1994). *Wherever You Go There You Are: Mindfulness Meditation in Everyday Life.* New York: Hyperion.

Schneider, W., and A. D. Fisk. (1982). "Dual task automatic and control processing: Can it be done without cost?" *Journal of Experimental Psychology: Learning, Memory, and Cognition,* 8, 261–278. This shows the reduced performance of doing two jobs at once as opposed to one.

Wickens, C. D., and J. G. Hollands. (2000). *Engineering Psychology and Human Performance* (3rd ed.). Upper Saddle River, N.J.: Prentice Hall.

CHAPTER 2: FEEL GREAT AT WORK

There is mounting evidence that positive attitudes and emotions improve both personal well-being and job performance. Over the last ten years there has been a huge increase in research into happiness and well-being. This trend has been described as "positive psychology," which is a movement led by Dr. Martin Seligman and

SCIENCE

represented by the positive psychology center – www.positive psychology.org. According to the website, "Positive Psychology is the scientific study of optimal human functioning" and is focused on generating tools and techniques for both home and work. With this in mind, we have provided a method for accessing positive states and developing positive attitudes, emotions, and behaviors.

One of the most researched attributes in this field is optimism. There is strong evidence to show that optimistic people are more successful. In his book *Learned Optimism,* Martin Seligman refers to a major study he conducted with insurance agents at Met Life. He administered a test for optimism to the agents, and the results showed that those agents in the less optimistic half were twice as likely to resign as those who were in the more optimistic half. Moreover, the agents in the top 25 percent sold twice as much as the agents from the bottom 25 percent.

Yet optimism can also be a matter of life and death. Harvard professor Laura Kubzansky conducted a survey of 1,300 men over ten years and found that men who labeled themselves optimistic had half the incidence of heart disease of those who did not.

References

Kubzansky, L. D., D. Sparrow, P. Vokonas, and I. Kawachi. (2001). "Is the glass half empty or half full: A prospective study of optimism and coronary heart disease in the normative aging study." *Psychosomatic Medicine,* 63, 910–916.

Seligman, Martin. (1990). *Learned Optimism.* NY: Pocket Books.

CHAPTER 3: ACT WITH CONFIDENCE

In this chapter we describe how to overcome anxieties, worries, and fears that sabotage your performance and sense of well-being. You learned how to regulate and manage your moods and achieve "emotional stability," which is also one of the big five personality factors. Some psychologists believe emotional stability is the most important dimension of happiness and is strongly correlated to life satisfaction (Hills and Argyle 2001).

Emotional stability refers to our degree of calmness, confidence, and level-headedness. It is contrasted to neuroticism, which is a high level of anxiety, depression, and mood swings. Such stability is particularly important for managing stress effectively and dealing with major periods of change and uncertainty.

We believe that we are always engaged in "self talk," and the quality of this self talk is a major factor in determining the quality of our lives. Throughout our book, we provide focus phrases which are positive replacements for negative self-talk. By improving our self-talk we improve our thoughts, and by changing our thoughts we improve our attitudes, behavior, and, ultimately, our results.

Our techniques are similar to those used by Cognitive Therapy, which is a very popular method used by therapists to help their clients manage their moods by managing their thoughts. Over many years, cognitive therapy has proven that if we change our thinking we can start to change our attitudes and let go of worries and anxieties. Moreover, this is supported by research which shows that when such therapy is combined with medication for treating depression, it is more effective than medication on its own.

SCIENCE

References

Hills, P. and M. Argyle. (2001). "Emotional stability as a major dimension of happiness." *Personality and Individual Differences,* 31, 1357–1364.

Jarrett, R. B., D. Kraft, J. Doyle, et al. (2001). "Preventing recurrent depression using cognitive therapy with and without a continuation phase: A randomized clinical trial." *Silver Arch Gen Psychiatry,* 58(4): 381–388.

Keller, M.B., J. P. McCullough, D. N. Klein, et al. (2000). "A comparison of nefazadone, the Cognitive Behavioral Analysis System of Psychotherapy and their combination for the treatment of chronic depression." *New England Journal of Medicine,* 322, 1462–1470.

Robertson, I. T., and M. Smith. (2001). "Personnel selection." *Journal of Occupational and Organisational Psychology,* 74(4): 441–72.

Salgado, J. (1997). "Emotional stability – high predictor of job performance: The five factor model of personality and job performance in the European community." *Journal of Applied Psychology,* 82, 30–43.

Tett, R. P., D. N. Jackson, and M. Rothstein. (1991). "Personality measures as predictors of job performance: A meta-analytic review." *Personnel Psychology,* 44, 703–742.

CHAPTER 4: COMMUNICATE WITH EMPATHY

When we judge others, we are making faulty assumptions about their behavior and personalities. There are a number of psychological theories associated with this phenomenon.

One is *stereotyping,* in which we make generalized judgments about others based on characteristics such as gender, race, education, or religion. This leads to misunderstanding and even conflict at work.

Another facet of judgment is the *fundamental attribution error,* which occurs when we believe people make mistakes or behave inappropriately because they are fundamentally bad or flawed in some way; while at the same time the judgers believe that their own mistakes are down to situational factors, such as pressure from others rather than because of their own character deficiencies. So we will tend to judge others who fail to complete a task as lazy, while seeing our own failure to complete a task as due to overload or events beyond our control.

In this chapter we help the reader become aware of these processes and replace them with a more empowering and useful method of non-judgment. Then, once we have developed in this area, we can start to develop our emotional intelligence (EI), which is our ability to be empathetic and build relationships with others. Not only does emotional intelligence improve your satisfaction and your performance at work, it is also evident that more employers are looking for people with high levels of EI.

For an overview of the research linking emotional intelligence and job performance, see "The Business Case for Emotional Intelligence" by Gary Cherniss at Rutgers University: www.eiconsortium.org/research/business_case_for_ei.pdf.

References

Goleman, D. (1998). *Working with Emotional Intelligence.* New York: Bantam Books.

Goleman, Daniel, Richard Boyatzis, and Annie McKee. (2002). *Primal Leadership.* Harvard Business School Press.

Robbins, Stephen P. (2003). *Organizational Behavior.* Upper Saddle

SCIENCE

River, N.J.: Prentice Hall. There is a good overview of stereotypes, the fundamental attribution error, and selective perception in chapter 5.

CHAPTER 5: BOOST YOUR SELF-ESTEEM

Self-esteem is a much-used term that has a wide range of meanings. It seems obvious that liking and accepting ourselves are valuable emotions. But what is self-esteem and what effect does it have on our performance at work?

We have highlighted two elements of self-esteem which are significant to job satisfaction and job performance. First is the concept of *self-efficacy,* which is our belief about our ability to achieve specific levels of performance and also have influence over our lives. According to Bandura (1997), who first promoted the idea, "perceived self-efficacy refers to beliefs in one's capabilities to organize and execute the courses of action required to produce given attainments" (p. 3). And research has shown that individuals who are high in self-efficacy achieve higher levels of job satisfaction and job performance. Moreover, high self-efficacy is also positively correlated to stress reduction (Jex et al. 2001).

The second concept is *locus of control* (Rotter 1966), which is a belief about the level of control that an individual has over his life. A person with a high *external locus of control* will tend to believe in the primary role of external circumstances, such as other people, luck, or fate. A person with a high *internal locus of control* will tend to believe that they are in charge of their lives and are responsible for their own destiny. Studies show that if you have a high internal locus of control you are more likely to be effective at work (Blau 1993).

References

Bandura, A. (1997). *Self-Efficacy: The Exercise of Control*. New York: Freeman.

Blau, G. (1993). "Testing the relationship of locus of control to different performance dimensions." *Journal of Occupational and Organizational Psychology,* 66, 125–138.

Jex, S. M., P. D. Bliese, S. Buzzell, and J. Primeau. (2001). "The impact of self-efficacy on stressor-strain relations: Coping style as an explanatory mechanism." *Journal of Applied Psychology,* 86, 401–409.

Judge, T. A., and J. E. Bono. (2001). "Relationship of core self-evaluations traits – self-esteem, generalized self-efficacy, locus of control, and emotional stability – with job satisfaction and job performance: A meta-analysis." *Journal of Applied Psychology,* 86, 80–92.

Rotter, J. (1996). "Generalized expectancies for internal versus external control of reinforcements." *Psychological Monographs,* 80(609), all.

CHAPTER 6: STIMULATE CREATIVE BREAKTHROUGHS

In this chapter, we show you how to create the right conditions for being creative and flexible. By taking charge of your moment-to-moment attention, you can reduce stress and relax into a state where creativity is encouraged.

Creativity is a highly prized asset in organizations. The ability to innovate and find creative solutions is often the most important

SCIENCE

advantage employees and organizations can enjoy in today's highly competitive marketplace.

Yet it is difficult to be creative in the modern workplace with so many stresses, interruptions, and demands. Studies have shown the importance of relaxing our minds to be more creative, including the correlation between practice of transcendental meditation and creativity (Travis 1979). Teresa Amabile, at Harvard Business School, is conducting a long-term study into the conditions for creativity at work. Her initial findings are that time pressures and distractions reduce creativity.

Moreover, creativity is not just a skill like writing or composing. It is also a state of mind, an ability to be flexible and change your beliefs and behaviors where appropriate. This is particularly important in today's volatile work environment, where there is so much change. Creative people who can be highly flexible and adaptive will flourish, whereas those who stay stuck in old habits will get left behind and also be prone to illness (Justice 1987).

References

Amabile, Teresa. See Fast Company, www.fastcompany.com/magazine/89/creativity.html, for a profile of her work.

Justice, Blair. (1987). *Who Gets Sick: Thinking and Health*. Houston, Texas: Peak Press.

Travis, F. T. (1979). "The TM technique and creativity: A longitudinal study of Cornell University undergraduates." *Journal of Creative Behavior*, 13(3): 169–180.

CHAPTER 7: GENERATE
TRUSTWORTHY DECISIONS

In this chapter we promote the idea of "wisdom" at work. By wisdom, we mean qualities such as intuition and strategic thinking that enable us to go beyond routine patterns of thinking.

The role of intuition in decision making is being increasingly studied (Lieberman 2000; Bayard 2001). Intuition is vital to making effective decisions because it derives from an unconscious awareness and understanding of complex situations (Khatri and Ng 2000). The authors have developed a decision-making process that integrates logic, experience, and intuition.

Strategic thinking is the ability to see the big picture and also the dynamic interrelationships between elements. For example, in business terms it is the ability to simultaneously understand your own needs, the needs of your team, your management, the organization as a whole, and your customers.

In another respect, wisdom is the ability to see yourself as part of a complex, dynamic system from multiple perspectives. This is similar to systems thinking and is featured in Peter Senge's book *The Fifth Discipline* (Senge 1990). Senge promotes the notion of becoming aware of and challenging our "mental models," which are the underlying assumptions we have that drive our behavior. He also recommends the practice of *double-loop learning* (Argyris 1976), which gives us a far deeper and richer analysis of our behavior and organizational behavior.

Single-loop learning is when we measure the results of our

SCIENCE

actions and readjust those actions accordingly, and double-loop learning is when we question and alter the beliefs and values that generated the action as well as measuring the results. So, in our context, trustworthy decisions are based on understanding a far wider range of factors and variables and looking at situations dynamically rather than statically.

And wisdom starts with self-awareness. It requires understanding ourselves better and being honest enough to recognize that much of our decision making is based on flawed assumptions and simple single-loop learning. Our ability to "think about how we think" has been called "Metacognition" (Flavell 1976) and is an important dimension of wisdom. Metacognition enables us to break free of routine, unconscious habits of thinking, and move to higher levels of insight and knowledge that enable us to be far more effective.

References

Argyris, C. (1976). *Increasing Leadership Effectiveness.* New York: Wiley.

Bayard, D. R. (2001). "Finding our balance: The investigation and clinical application of intuition." *Psychotherapy Theory, Research, Practice, Training: Special Issue,* 38, 97–106.

Flavell, J. H. (1976). "Metacognitive aspects of problem solving." In L. B. Resnick (ed.), *The Nature of Intelligence.* Hillsdale, N.J.: Erlbaum.

Khatri, N., and H. A. Ng. (2000). "The role of intuition in strategic decision making." *Human Relations,* 53, 57–86.

Liebermann, M. D. (2000). "Intuition: A social cognitive neuroscience approach." *Psychological Bulletin,* 126:109–137.

Senge, P. (1990). *The Fifth Discipline: The Art and Practice of the Learning Organization.* New York: Doubleday.

CHAPTER 8: ACT WITH INTEGRITY

Employees want to find ways of balancing their work and home lives, and there has been a big rise in corporate wellness programs, including training in yoga and meditation. They are also looking for ways to integrate their personal values into their occupations and for finding meaning at work (Hoar 2004). There has been an increasing interest in the notion of spirituality in the workplace, which refers not just to organized religion but also the role of personal values, ethics, and needs in organizational life.

More and more people come to work looking to satisfy more than their financial needs. They want to find a calling or a vocation. This explains the rise of interest in business ethics and corporate social responsibility (CSR). If we are able to earn money and do good, we will achieve major psychological benefits in addition to our salaries. Moreover, there is growing evidence that organizations that are serious about CSR are more successful (Orlitzky, Schmidt, and Rynes 2003).

Work is more than *doing* the job and *having* the rewards. It is also about *being* the person you want to be. Once we have satisfied our basic needs for employment, remuneration, and recognition, we are motivated by "self-actualization." Indeed, the self-actualized person at work brings together all the qualities we have been promoting in our book. They accept themselves and other people; they have a more accurate perception of reality and like to solve problems; they are more creative and spontaneous; they have deeper relationships with other people; and they have stronger values to which they are committed (Maslow 1968).

SCIENCE

References

Giacalone, R. A., and C. L. Jurkeiwocz (eds.). (2003). *Handbook of Workplace Spirituality and Organizational Performance.* Armonk, N.Y.: M.E. Sharpe.

Greenleaf, R. K. (1977). "Servant leadership: A journey into the nature of legitimate power and greatness." New York: Paulist Press.

His Holiness the Dalai Lama, Howard C. Cutler. (2003). *The Art of Happiness at Work.* New York: Riverhead Books.

Holbeche, Linda, and Nigel Springett. (2004). "In search of meaning in the workplace." Roffey Park Research Report UK, as reported in *Management Today* by Rebecca Hoar, May 2004.

Maslow, A. (1968). *Toward a Psychology of Being.* New York: Van Nostrand Reinhold.

Mitroff, Ian, and Elizabeth A. Denton. (1999). *Spiritual Audit of Corporate America.* San Francisco: Jossey-Bass.

Orlitzky, Marc, Frank L Schmidt, and Sara Rynes. (2003). "Corporate social and financial performance: A meta-analysis." *Organization Studies,* 24, 403–411.

ABOUT THE AUTHORS

Paul Hannam offers a unique perspective on how to achieve high levels of performance and personal fulfillment at work. He brings together a successful track record in three critical areas of expertise – as a very successful entrepreneur, management consultant, and lecturer at Oxford University. He is the owner and chairman of a corporation in the United Kingdom with annual sales of more than $20 million, and during the last 20 years, he has trained thousands of people in the business and nonprofit sectors. He has been hired to provide consultancy and training programs for some of the world's leading corporations, such as Barclays Bank, British Airways, HSBC, British Telecom, Canon, Fidelity Investments, Mars, Express Newspapers, and many more.

Paul lectured in organizational behavior, leadership, entrepreneurship, and change management at Oxford University, where he is an associate fellow. He was also an adjunct fellow of Linacre College from 2002 until 2005. His expertise covers a wide range of subjects, including psychology, motivation, leadership, strategy, change management, communication, sales, and marketing. He has a degree in history and international politics from Reading University in the UK and an MA in international politics from Carleton University in Canada. For more information, see Paul's website www.phannan.co.uk.

John Selby is a psychologist with thirty years experience developing these core mind-management techniques. He completed motivation and stress-reduction research at the National Institutes of Health and the Bureau of Research in Neurology and Psychiatry, and is the author of two dozen books on consciousness management. Founder and former CEO of The BrightMind Network and currently head of Consciousness Management Systems, John is a specialist in creating online experiential-instruction formats that deliver effective and affordable training to organizations throughout the world.

HAMPTON ROADS
PUBLISHING COMPANY, INC.

for the evolving human spirit

Thank you for reading *Take Charge of Your Mind*. Hampton Roads is proud to publish an extensive array of books on the topics discussed in this book—topics such as business, sales, motivation, and more. Please take a look at the following selection or visit us anytime on the web: www.hrpub.com.

Listening with Empathy
Creating Genuine Connections with Customers and Colleagues

John Selby

The companion book to *Take Charge of Your Mind*. Based on the principle that if you feel good, your clients will too, *Listening with Empathy* provides a simple yet astonishingly effective 4-step mood-boosting method for rapidly shifting from a negative to a *genuinely* positive mood at work and making authentic contact with customers and co-workers. As you hone your abilities to create strong bonds with others by making them feel truly listened to and appreciated, you'll find yourself increasingly confident, charismatic—and successful.

Trade cloth • 240 pages • ISBN 1-57174-514-9 • $19.95

Excuse Me, Your Job Is Waiting

Attract the Work You Want

Laura George

Excuse Me, Your Job Is Waiting approaches job hunting from Lynn Grabhorn's philosophy and applies the powerful Law of Attraction to getting a job. George captures the style and substance of Grabhorn's *Excuse Me, Your Life Is Waiting* and helps you identify the qualities you want in a job. You'll learn to flip the negative feelings ("the economy is terrible"; "I can't believe I got laid off"; "I'm too old") to positive ones and stay focused on drawing that perfect job to you. From an HR manager perspective, George helps you understand how powerful, positive feelings can help you land the job of your dreams.

Paperback • 312 pages • ISBN 978-1-57174-529-3 • $16.95

Hampton Roads Publishing Company

. . . for the evolving human spirit

HAMPTON ROADS PUBLISHING COMPANY publishes books on a variety of subjects, including metaphysics, spirituality, health, visionary fiction, and other related topics.

For a copy of our latest trade catalog, call toll-free, 800-766-8009, or send your name and address to:

HAMPTON ROADS PUBLISHING COMPANY, INC.
1125 STONEY RIDGE ROAD • CHARLOTTESVILLE, VA 22902
e-mail: hrpc@hrpub.com • www.hrpub.com